12-6

Erna's Life

Erna's Life

by Janice Whelan and Erna P. Roberts

Front Cover Illustration: *A painting by Astride.*

10 9 8 7 6 5 4 3 2 1

A catalogue record for this book is available from the Library of Congress.

ISBN: 978-1495941184

Contents

Erna Pauline Murmanis Roberts

Introduction

There is something rare and beautiful about Erna Pauline Roberts at age 96, clearly remembering and telling the events of the first third of her life, the years from 1917-1949. This is the life about which her daughters want to know. It is the past that Erna tried to block from her memory; a part of her life that she would not talk about for many years. For Erna, remembering her past was painful for what she had lost; the memory of a magical, happy and safe childhood. It was even more painful for her to remember what she had to do as a young wife and mother so that she and her children would survive their escape from Soviet dominated Latvia. This is one refugee's story, but it is the story that is repeated throughout history; the story of how war shatters and destroys the lives of the innocent, especially the women and children. Families are uprooted, homes destroyed, lives are lost. It is also the story of one refugee family's struggle to survive and their ultimate triumph against what seemed like insurmountable odds.

"Things happen for a reason" is a platitude that is often used to encourage an individual to accept what life has thrown at them without really seeing the connecting and repeating patterns. That platitude took on new meaning as Erna remembered and described the patterns that were interwoven to create the tapestry of her life. Perhaps Erna became aware of that in her retelling, "Luck just seemed to follow me.", as she described events that she may not have perceived as lucky when they were happening. For example, there were times, during her childhood education in Latvia, when she was not too happy to be studying German and English; and times when she was delighted to learn embroidery. She remembered learning to knit in her home economics class and how much she hated trying to knit that mitten. Why would she think, as she learned these skills, that they would be among the instruments which insured her survival, and would eventually bring her to the United States of America?

Erna said that her new life began when she left Ellis Island with her husband, Arijs Freimanis, and four daughters; Astride, Rudite, Zaiga, and Inara. She carried a medium sized suitcase which held her few belongings. Astride, the eldest daughter, carried her back pack containing the children's clothing. This back pack had accompanied them from Latvia to the United States.

The four little girls were ages 9-3. They brought with them the traditional national costumes of Latvia that Erna had sewn from army blankets during her final days as a refugee. Tucked away in her suitcase was a picture of the four little girls in their costumes, honoring their Latvian heritage, a heritage that the Soviets tried to obliterate. Her husband's Uncle John, with the help of the Quaker Church, had made their immigration possible. A representative of that church was waiting for them at Ellis Island. Eventually, through the Quakers, they found their new life and home, first, on a farm near Clinton and then in a little house in Tecumseh, Michigan. That is where Erna insisted on leaving her story, because that is where her daughters' individual stories would begin.

Part One

Janice Whelan and Erna P. Roberts

1.

Beginning Her Story

ERNA SAT ALONE in a quiet room at her daughter Astride's house. A cassette recorder had been set up for her and a kind, patient voice could be heard on the recording explaining to her how to start and stop the recorder. She began, "I am doing this for my girls because this is what they want to know. It is a very hard thing for me to do".

She described her memory search "The telling was like opening a data bank in my mind. Now I lie in bed at night and all of those memories come flooding back."

Erna's story takes place from 1917-1949. The majority of that time, 1921-1939, is set in Latvia. The years 1921-1939, were a good time for her family and for Latvia in general. While the rest of Europe was sinking into depression, Latvia's economy was prospering. For the time being the Latvians were free of Russian and German domination. Unfortunately, that prosperity and flourishing economy would make Latvia even more attractive to financially struggling Russia and Germany once World War Two was underway. The Latvians cherished their new independence with a written constitution. In the Latvian consciousness this period was known as "the golden era of progress and achievement, the second awakening." (The Library of Congress Country Studies, Latvia Independence, 1918-1940)

Erna said that she had everything a girl could want. "I see that little girl dressed in a white pinafore, ribbons in her long hair, wearing cream colored shoes. Those high button shoes are dirty from the puddles she could not avoid on her way to the Easter swings in the field... So many, many things are coming back," Memories that she did not think about as she struggled to escape the Russians and keep her daughters safe began to flood her mind. Until now, those memories would have been too much to bear.

2.

1921-1923

Hello Latvia

HER VERY FIRST MEMORY began when she and her parents, Janis and Pauline Murmanis, left Estonia. The year was 1921 and WWI was over. Erna was four years old, a little girl in a pinafore, with hair ribbons adorning her long braids. She and her father, Janis, and mother, Pauline, were returning to their native Latvia. They had left Estonia, where her father had learned stone masonry; building breakers in Tallinn, on the Baltic Sea Coastline. This was her father's education, even though it was difficult to learn a trade and support a family at the same time. While there, on June 25, 1917, Erna was born.

There would be many more train rides for Erna, but this one took them to a happy time, because she and her family were coming home. It was a good time to be returning to Latvia. The Latvia-Soviet Peace Treaty had been signed On August 11, 1920. "Russia unreservedly recognizes the independence and sovereignty of the Latvian State and voluntarily and forever renounces all sovereign rights over the Latvian people." Latvia's new independence lasted for a brief 20 years and was referred to as the "second awakening", a golden era of progress and achievement.

Erna described Latvia during those years as a beautiful country, edged by the unbroken Baltic Sea coastline. It was a flower filled, fairytale world of forests, castles, manors, and majestic estates inland. Latvia, Lithuania, and Estonia have always been coveted by other countries such as Russia, Germany, Poland and Sweden, because of their unbroken coastline on the Baltic Sea. Since the Baltic Sea never freezes it was very important for shipping. Consequently, these three small countries throughout their history have been dominated by other larger, more powerful countries. Yet, during those years of Erna's childhood and young adulthood Latvia thrived with its independence.

After their train had pulled into the station in Ligatne, Janis left Erna and Pauline waiting on the platform while he went to collect their belongings; clothing, dishes, tools, blankets, perhaps some furniture. To his dismay, he discovered that everything that they had brought with them had been stolen. Distraught, Janis returned to his wife and daughter, looked at his family and said, "They have taken everything that I own but I still have my daughter." Sadly this statement foreshadowed a continuing theme in their lives.

Eight years later Erna and her family returned to Estonia for a vacation. They stayed at an inn and visited the places where her father had worked; especially the sea walls where her father had learned masonry work. It was on that visit that her parents also took her to a cemetery and showed her where another brother was buried. He was born in 1914, and died shortly after his first birthday. This was the first time that Erna had heard of her brother, Janis Volmanis Murmanis.

Life at the Manor

There are castles near Ligatne and around each castle are manorial estates with large manor houses, owned by the German barons and baronesses. Although the Germans returned some of the land to Latvia, and the Latvian government divided this land among the people who had worked for the estates, the German owned manorial estates continue to dominate rural Latvia today.

Pauline's Uncle Peteris (her grandfather's brother) worked at Rama Manor, outside the Ligatne area, as a horseman. Her uncle told Janis that he, Pauline, and Erna could live with him and his wife. They shared an apartment consisting of two rooms and a kitchen.

Janis immediately found work in construction, due to the immense amount of building and remodeling taking place in Latvia after its independence. During the day Pauline assisted with the chores around the manor house. In the evening she helped with the milking in the barn. The little girl, Erna, would sit on the steps with nothing to do, but watch. On one of those times, while her mama was milking, Erna was sitting outside of the dairy just waiting.

A workman walked up to her and said, "I will give you some candy if you will take the milking girls' shoes and hide them in the bushes. It will be a good joke to play on them."

Erna had no idea why he would want her to do that, but she loved candy, so she nodded in agreement, quietly took the shoes, and hid them in the bushes nearby. When her mama and the rest of the girls were finished with the milking they came out and discovered that all of their shoes had mysteriously disappeared.

On another day a little neighbor girl came to play. She was carrying a doll. Erna was very happy to play with this new friend and especially her doll, since she had never had a doll of her own. They decided to wash the doll's clothes in a nearby pond.

Of course they needed soap and Erna exclaimed, "I can get us some soap. I know where my mama keeps her soap."

She quickly ran into the apartment, found the soap, and brought it to the pond where her new friend and doll were waiting. They removed the doll's clothes and began to scrub them in the pond. Unfortunately, when the soap was wet it became slippery and jumped right out of Erna's little hands, sinking out of reach, into the pond. That was a time when Erna first learned that if you do something wrong you have to admit it. Her mama was not happy when she needed to use the bar of soap and could not find it anywhere. Erna had to tell her what had happened to that soap. She also learned about consequences since she could no longer play with the neighbor girl and her doll. She was back sitting on the step, watching.

Another time, while she lived at the manor, Erna noticed her aunt's pretty geranium flower pot that was sitting on the shelf in the kitchen. She stretched, stood on her tiptoes, and then as she cautiously reached and picked it up to inspect it more closely, the flower pot slipped out of her hands, fell to the floor, and cracked. She tried unsuccessfully to hide the damage by turning it so that the crack was facing the wall. Her aunt, of course, figured out what had happened, and reminded Erna that when you do something wrong you must tell someone.

A Walk In The Park

Close by the manor there was a park with rose gardens and paths to walk among the fragrant, colorful flowers. One Sunday Erna was dressed in her starched white pinafore. She had ribbons festively tied in her hair and high buttoned shoes on her feet. She was feeling quite proud and independent since she had buttoned those shoes all by herself. On this warm sunny day there was not a cloud in the sky. Erna noticed the Barons and Baronesses, who were all decked out in their Sunday finery, also walking in the park, carrying opened umbrellas over their heads as if it was raining. The umbrellas were not ordinary black umbrellas, but instead were all of the colors of the rainbow. She could not imagine why they were all carrying those pretty and colorful umbrellas, since there was not a drop of rain coming down from the sky. As the elegant ladies and their gentlemen strolled by, she stared in puzzled amazement.

Later, she asked her aunt, "Why do they have umbrellas when it is not raining?"

Erna's aunt explained, "Those are not umbrellas. They are parasols. The ladies carry them to keep the sun off of their faces."

Since it was such a nice day and she was all dressed up, Erna then decided that it would be good idea to continue her walk and visit Aunt Anna who lived about 35 miles away in Riga.

As she was walking by the gardens, one of the Baronesses stopped her and asked, "Little girl, where are you going all dressed up so nicely?"

Erna replied, "I am going to visit my Aunt Anna in Riga."

The Baroness gently took her hand and said, "Perhaps we should go back and let your mama know where you are going. She might want to go with you."

Of course that put a stop to Erna's future walks in the park alone.

On Their Own In Ligatne

Janis's construction job was renovating a huge manor house, Krimulda Manor, to become a vocational academy. It was going to be used as an agricultural school, which would provide training for young Latvian men. Now that Latvia was independent the academy would give these young men a fresh start and a vocation. Often Erna and her mama would walk to her papit's work site, bringing him his lunch.

Far left, Grandfather Vanags. Erna between Janis and Pauline Murmanis

In the evening she would anxiously wait for Papit, her father, to come home from work. She would run to meet him, knowing that there would always be a candy in his pocket for her. This did not make her mama happy and she would tell Erna, "Eating so much candy, you are not going to have any teeth.

Because her father had a lot of construction work it was not long before they were able to afford to move into their own apartment, on the second story, above a store in Ligatne. Erna was very excited to see what it would be like. When they arrived there, Erna found that it had two rooms and a kitchen, which seemed very spacious and luxurious at that time.

Next to their apartment was a woodworker's shop. Erna enjoyed visiting the woodworker because he gave her scraps of wood to use as building blocks. With the blocks she would build houses and cities with roads and bridges. This kept her occupied for hours. On one occasion, after building many houses with her blocks, she became very sleepy. She looked around the shop and noticed that there was a long wooden box with its lid propped open. It was just the right place for a little girl to crawl into, curl up, and take a nap.

Later that afternoon, as supper time approached, her parents became concerned because they could not find her in the usual places. Everyone began frantically to look for her. Perhaps all of the commotion and confusion woke Erna and she sleepily climbed out of her box, not knowing that it was a coffin. When she showed her parents where she had been, they informed her that, sadly, there would be no more visiting the woodworker's shop. As Erna said, "It was back to sitting on the step, watching the world go by, with nothing to do."

3.

1924-1926

Changes At Home

BY 1924, JANIS'S construction business had grown considerably. He
had decided to expand his business into woodworking; opening a factory
which produced doors, windows and elaborate trim. He also could afford
to buy his family their own house in Ligatne, located a short walking dis-
tance from Erna's school. Janis was becoming one of the most respected,
successful men in Latvia. Consequently, little Erna's life, like a fairytale,
started to change and she became almost a "princess" in her Latvian
town.

School opened up a new and wonderful life for Erna because she
finally had a chance to meet other children. For the most part she was
a very happy little girl, except when she was walking to school wearing
the long scratchy, woolen stockings, lovingly made for her by Aunt Alida,
cousin Arvid's mother. Since the itchy stockings were necessary to help
keep her legs warm, Erna solved the problem by wearing cotton stockings
under the wool ones, which helped to alleviate the itching. She admits
that she still cannot stand to wear wool.

Eventually Janis bought her a bicycle so that she could ride to school. On the day that it was to be delivered her father gave her a slip of paper and told her to go to the train station to pick up her new bicycle. Bursting with excitement, she ran all of the way there and handed the paper to the station attendant, who then left to look for her bicycle.

"Here it is." he said as a he wheeled out her new bicycle, "It is yours."

There was one small problem. Erna had never ridden a bicycle. With a great deal of embarrassment, she slowly walked her new bicycle all of the way home. Not lacking in determination, in a short while she was confidently riding that bicycle to school and eventually to work.

School Days

Erna attended grade school for eight years. The school's morning would begin with religious instruction, including singing hymns and learning Bible verses. Since the churches were too far away for the children to go there every day for catechism, religion was taught in the school. In second grade Erna began to learn a foreign language, choosing English over Russian and German.

Sometimes in the winter, during recess, the children would go sledding.

Erna was a bit hesitant to try it but her friends persuaded her, "Come on, give it a try! You will love it!" they coaxed.

Reluctantly she climbed on the sled, and someone gave her a push. The sled raced down the icy hill, suddenly veered off of the track and slid into the not quite frozen creek. An extremely unhappy Erna trudged back to the school with wet feet and dripping clothes.

The principal called Pauline, who immediately brought dry shoes and clothes for her cold, completely drenched daughter. Without another choice, a very disappointed little girl changed into her dry clothes. She had hoped that she might have been given the rest of the day off to compensate for her stressful situation. After her sledding experience, if someone would ask her to go sledding again, she would look crossly at them and reply with an emphatic "No thank you!"

Although she recalled that the teachers were very strict, Erna admitted to being a little rebellious as a student. "I liked to do the things I liked."

History was her favorite subject. Even though math was easy for her, it was not one of the subjects that she particularly liked to do. One time she just did not feel like doing her math assignment, so she didn't do it. Consequently, the teacher kept her after school to finish her work. After he had her situated at her desk with the work she needed to finish, he left her working alone in the classroom while he went hunting. When he finished hunting, having forgotten all about Erna, he went home.

Erna finished her assignment and then waited and waited for her teacher to return. Finally she rested her head on the desk and fell asleep.

When she did not come home from school on time Janis and Pauline became very worried. It turned dark so quickly in the winter and they didn't like Erna to walk home alone. They also knew that she was very frightened to walk in the dark, past the cemetery, that was between the school and their home. Janis called the principal, who returned to the school and found her sound asleep at her desk.

The principal called the teacher, who was embarrassed that he had forgotten all about Erna, and said, "Don't worry, I will go to the school and accompany her home."

Quite certain that the teacher would be in a lot of trouble for leaving her alone in the classroom and forgetting all about her, Erna was surprised and disappointed that her father was instead angry with her for not doing her schoolwork. To add insult to injury, he even invited the neglectful teacher, who just happened to be his hunting buddy, to stay for some refreshments.

His daughter's education was very important to Janis. He planned for her to go to business school and in order to do that she would need good grades to be accepted there. In contrast to her father's plans, Erna had always dreamed of studying piano at the Conservatory. She had been taking piano lessons and hoped to one day be a piano teacher.

"Absolutely not." Her father declared. "Music school is out. You are going to Volola Academy, to business school, so that you can help me in my business."

Because her brother was nine years younger, their father needed Erna to get her business degree. He couldn't wait another nine years for her brother to catch up. Tucking away her own dreams, Erna was a little heartbroken but would never consider questioning or going against her father's wishes.

A Larger Family

Erna's maternal grandfather, Janis Vanags, was a horseman on a large manor. He was given permission to live there for his lifetime. After his wife's early death, when Pauline was only five years old and her brother Peteris was just two, he began raising his two children at the manor, with the help of the manor maids.

Grandfather would often come to visit his daughter and her family at their new house. On one of his visits he told Janis, "I would come to live with you if you had a horse,"

Her father replied, "Where would I keep a horse?"

Stable

Later on her parents discussed the possibility of Grandfather living with them and agreed that it could be very helpful to have him move in. He would be another person to help look after Erna if they were away. They decided to build a stable and buy Grandfather a horse. The stable would also have a wine cellar for Pauline's homemade wine. It was 1926, when he finally came to live with them.

On their property there was a field with an enormous old oak tree. Every spring the storks would return from their winter migration and perch in that tree. Erna's grandfather, while gazing at the oak tree whose massive branches were crowded with those long legged birds, wondered out loud, "Maybe those storks will bring Erna a baby brother."

Janis Murmanis

Hearing him say this, his little grand daughter was quite puzzled as to how that could happen.

Several months passed by. Pauline had been away for three days and Erna was worried and wondered where her mother could be.

Ligatne House

On that third day Papit told Erna, "Hurry and get ready. We are going to Riga."

Erna wondered why. She thought that perhaps they might be going to visit her Aunt Anna who lived there.

They boarded the train and when they arrived in Riga they walked to a strange building. Janis explained, "This is a hospital."

In the hospital waiting room there was a table covered with many books. Her father told her, "Sit down here and look at the books. I will be back in a minute."

Pauline and children

As she sat looking through the books she could hear a baby crying and wondered what was happening. When she found out that the cries were coming from her new baby brother, Zigfrids, she asked, "Where are the storks?"

Erna was not expecting this big change in her life and had mixed feelings. She was at first happy and then later, not so happy, since she always had to look after her little brother. She had acquired an obligation, since her mother would tell her to listen for her brother's crying and come tell her.

4.

1927-1931

Growing Up,

A Girl With Many Interests

REFLECTING ON A TIME when there was no television or radio for entertainment in their home, Erna remembered playing bingo and checkers with her grandfather. At school she took a home making class and was taught knitting and sewing, but what she really loved to do was embroider. Her parents employed two maids. One of the maids would embroider in the evening when she had finished her work. This maid kindly agreed to teach Erna how to embroider. She traced a daisy on a piece of cloth for her eager student to stitch.

"I thought that I had gold in my hand as I worked so hard to make that embroidered daisy," she recalled.

A visit from Aunt Anna (actually her mother's cousin) who lived in Riga, was anxiously anticipated since that aunt would bring Erna colored pencils, water colors and paper dolls. She and her little neighbor friend would spend fun filled hours cutting out the paper doll clothes so that they could stylishly dress their paper dolls. She also remembered a game that they would play with small stones, similar to games with marbles that are played here in the United States.

Yet, Erna, as a little girl, had a resourcefulness and independent streak which would certainly serve her well as an adult, even though it caused her father much consternation. While still in grade school she thought that it would be nice to earn a little spending money.

Her aunt Alida had a job at a nearby farm weeding the vegetable gardens and told Erna, "You can come with me and weed at the farm."

That sounded like a good plan since she enjoyed gardening, so she agreed to work with her aunt. They went to the farm and spent the day weeding the garden. When they finished, at the end of the day, the owner did not pay them, but promised to give them their money soon. Deep down, Erna probably knew that her father would not approve of her job so she failed to mention it to him.

Consequently, when the owner ran into Janis in town and informed him, "I have some money for your daughter for the time she weeded for me," Janis was not happy.

He emphatically told Erna, "Under no circumstances are you to ever again work on a farm weeding!"

To soften his ultimatum he promised "When you can ride your bike really well, you can take a trip to your Uncle Karlis at Unger Manor to pick apples in the fall."

When that time finally came she took the train to Cesis and then rode her bicycle to his orchard. Her uncle found her to be a good worker. She climbed the trees to pick the apples and then she and Cousin Imants, uncle Karlis' nephew, would pack them in boxes to be sold at the market. At the market she wore a big apron with a pocket in front to hold the money, as she helped her uncle sell the apples. At twelve years of age, she was quite young to be in charge of the money. Erna came to realize that perhaps her father wanted her to understand at an early age about hard work and that there were no handouts in life.

As one of the most important men in Latvia, there were apparently correct appearances that Janis needed to maintain. Unfortunately, his "little princess" had her own ideas, which sometimes caused him much aggravation. Erna was very interested in visiting a beauty shop in town and getting to know the young women who worked there. She had thought a lot about getting her long braids cut and wanted to talk to them about getting her hair cut and what styles they would recommend. For some reason, Janis thought that they would be a bad influence on his daughter and had forbidden her from hanging around the beauty shop.

One morning, after his lecture on staying away from the beauty shop, Erna watched her father as he walked briskly, briefcase in hand, to the train station. Assuming that he was going to be out of town for the day, she hopped on her bike and headed for the forbidden beauty shop.

As she happily chatted with the hair dressers, she did not notice her father storm into the shop. "Where is your bike?" he asked.

She retrieved her bike and they slowly walked the bike home. Not a word was spoken the entire way back. When they arrived home he took her to his office.

"Didn't I tell you not to go the beauty shop?" he asked in his sternest voice.

" Yes," she replied truthfully, "but I want to get my hair cut and I wanted to talk to them about that."

"Never." he replied, "You will not cut your hair." Consequently, even when Erna went away to business school, it was with a long braid wrapped around her head.

When Erna had finished business school and was working in her father's business, she was allowed to drive his prized motorcycle to help her quickly travel from one factory to another. This motorcycle was a shiny black, with blue trim, BMW 350. Because she became very adept at handling it, her cousin Arvid and another worker encouraged her to enter a motorcycle race while Janis was out of town on business.

"We will get your bike ready for the race", they coaxed. "All you will have to do is show up. It will be a lot of fun and maybe you will win a prize." Erna was easily convinced, as she thought to herself, "What would be the harm? No one will ever know." She also admitted that she still quietly resented that she had to give up her career plans in music and thought that she could at least have this.

Shortly after that, on a warm Sunday morning, with Janis conveniently out of town, Erna rode the motorcycle to the nearby field where the race would take place. Wearing a skirt and no helmet, she raced the straight away, came in second, and was presented with an amber ashtray. Although she never smoked, that ashtray was always displayed proudly on her desk. As she proudly accepted her trophy she turned around to face the spectators. There in the crowd her eyes caught sight of her father. They stared at each other for what seemed like an eternity.

Finally, Janis approached her and said, "Your cousin will drive the motorcycle home. You will come with me."

At home, Erna earned another trip to her father's office where she was lectured about her impropriety. Janis then decreed "that is the last time that you will ride that motorcycle."

Holiday Fun

Latvia always has been a country of many celebrations and every Latvian makes time to celebrate. Easter, Name Day, Janis Day, Harvest Celebrations, Christmas, New Year's Day and birthdays were the holidays that Erna awaited with great anticipation.

One favorite time of celebration for Erna was her father's Name Day, Janis Day, on June 24. June 24 is the date when Janis appears on the Latvian calendar. On that date, friends, neighbors, and family would visit all of the houses where someone held the name of Janis. The celebrants would bring wreaths of birch leaves and wildflowers. They would then place a wreath over Janis's head before partying on to the next house. All guests were welcome and no individual invitation was required. An abundance of traditional food, which might include a delicious pork roast, sliced and served with gravy, was prepared and presented on large tables for the guests to enjoy. The music of guitars, harmonicas and singing would fill the air. The centerpiece of the Name Day table was the traditional Name Day cake, Klingeris, a saffron cake made with raisins and almonds, baked in the shape of a pretzel. For Erna and her family, this celebration would become a two-day party since Erna's birthday followed on June 25.

On Easter, gigantic swings would be assembled in a field near the village. The children would walk through the mud and the puddles to get to those wonderful swings.

Everyone would decorate eggs to exchange, with prizes for the most beautifully decorated. The procedure for decorating the Easter eggs is a special Latvian tradition that Erna shares with her children and grandchildren. The procedure is to wrap the eggs with dried onion skins, leaves and flowers in a tightly tied cloth, and then cook them. When they unwrap them the patterns of the enclosed items show on the amber colored eggs.

Janis generously bought musical instruments for the community orchestra. The Latvian people loved their celebrations, which would become even more festive with a live orchestra. The orchestra would play for the summer dances in the fields and for the autumn festivals and bazaars. Her mother's woman's group each year organized a charity ball to help the elderly and the children, especially at Christmas time, and of course the orchestra would provide the music for that event.

The Harvest Celebration was at the end of autumn at the Community Center. Erna's father had renovated Palmala Manor and donated it to the village of Ligatne, as a community center. There would be a bazaar with many different handmade items; knitted socks and scarves, or intricately embroidered scarves and handkerchiefs. Each item would have a number and drawings would be held to see who would win them. In the evening everyone looked forward to the dance.

When the celebrations included dancing, Erna loved to watch her mother dance and would sometimes join her. Pauline was a naturally happy, joyous woman and danced with many partners. Janis was not one of those partners. Since he didn't care to dance, he was content to sit with the men, while they all enjoyed their beer.

Erna described her parents as very caring, generous people. Perhaps it was because they had come from hardship themselves. Janis's stepmother, his father's third wife, was so mean to him that at the young age of 7 he ran away to live with his Uncle Peteris and his cousin Karlis at Unger Manor. This uncle and cousin became just like a father and brother to Janis.

Because of this experience when he was a young boy, Janis had a special place in his heart for the orphanage in town. He knew what it was like to feel unloved and unwanted, which is why he made large donations to ensure that the orphanage would be able to provide the children with a safe place to live. Every Christmas the orphanage would invite Erna's family to a tree lighting ceremony.

At one of these ceremonies there was a 17 year old boy who caught Janis's eye. He told Erna, "Go and talk to that boy and see if he has any family."

She walked up to the boy and asked him, "What is your name?"

He replied, "Yaniz"

"Will your family be visiting you tonight?" she asked.

"No, I do not have any family," he replied sadly.

Some of the children stayed at the orphanage because their parents could not take care of them at home. Their parents would still come to visit them, eventually hoping to bring them back home when their circumstances would improve.

Since Yaniz did not have any family that might be able to take care of him, Janis went over to him and asked, "Would you like to come live with my family?"

Zigfrids

Yaniz smiled and gratefully nodded that he would.

The arrangements were quickly made with the people in charge of the orphanage and Yaniz returned home with Erna's family that same evening. Yaniz worked as a wood worker for Janis, who had plans to send him to trade school. Unfortunately the war disrupted these plans. During the German occupation of Latvia the German

Erna

Army conscripted Yaniz, along with over 200,000 Latvian men, into its service. Erna found out much later that he had been killed in battle.

Christmas was primarily a time for family, a time to spend with aunts and uncles from the city. It was also a time when Janis would provide money and food to his father's less fortu-nate relatives. Erna remembered an elderly man who appealed to her father for as-sistance every Christmas and of course was never denied.

In their parlor there would stand a freshly cut Christmas tree with real burning candles clipped to its branches. Miraculously, that tree never caught on fire. On Christmas Eve her grandfather would transport them in a horse drawn sleigh to church. Then on Christmas Day they would find their gifts under the tree, knowing that Santa had brought them.

Janis and Pauline

Erna recalled that she and her brother would each get one gift, perhaps a dress for her and new shoes for him. Before they could open their gift they were required to sing a song or recite a Bible verse. Sometimes a neighbor, dressed up like Santa, would stop by to bring them candy.

On New Year's Eve the family would pour molten lead into cold water to form shapes that perhaps might reveal their future. Ironically, Erna still has her piece that formed into a ship. Years later she would experience passage on ships that would change her life. Then on New Year's Day they would relax and quietly contemplate on what the New Year would bring.

An Introduction To The Factory

At around the age of ten Erna spent most of her time working in the business. There were no more paper dolls, but instead, her free time was spent at the office working with the book keeper, who was a retired policeman. First, he showed her how to sharpen all of the pencils with a sharp knife. Then he taught her all about the lumber that they used and how to measure it. As soon as a load of lumber would arrive she would be the first one to run through the doorway in order to figure it out. Erna still has the abacus-like calculator that she used when working on the accounts with the book keeper. It was tucked away in a package that her mother had saved for her and gave to her many years later. The future little executive would also keep track of who was late to work and who did not do their job correctly.

Watchman's gate to Ligatne house and factory

Local transportation

Family Values

As Erna described the Latvia of her childhood, "So many things are coming back," she remembered a happy childhood with loving but strict parents who kept them safe. She and her brother would never talk back or argue with her parents, it was just not heard of. There was no shouting, just listening, even though there were times when she disagreed.

Due to their standing in the community, Pauline was expected to do an immense amount of entertaining. To alleviate some of this burden, they eventually hired two maids to work in their home. One of the maids worked in the house and the other took care of the washing, the bath house and the gardens. Even though they had two maids Erna was still expected to make her bed every day. That was the rule. One morning she decided that bed making was a waste of her time and that the maid should make her bed for her. After all they did have two maids, and wasn't that what maids were supposed to do?

It was of utmost importance to Janis and Pauline that they raise their children to be considerate of others. When Janis found out about Erna's "new" attitude, he quickly put a stop to that line of thought.

"As long as you live in my house you will make your own bed," he informed her. "You have to learn to do these things. You may have climbed to the top of the ladder but you must know how to take care of yourself if you come back down that ladder."

Pauline Vanags Murmanis

Having struggled up the ladder himself he knew first hand that there were no guarantees in life. Her parents taught Erna to never look down on people who did not have as many possessions or opportunities as she did.

The workers in his factories and their families meant a lot to Janis. He kept track of their children and made sure that they had shoes to wear. Every Christmas he would invite them to a party at the factory. There would be gifts from Santa for each child and a gold watch for the workers who had worked there five years.

Besides spending many hours working for the community and his business, Janis was also involved in government and traveled all over Latvia making speeches. Many years later, when Erna returned to Latvia, an older gentleman introduced himself to her and recalled, "I will always remember your father running to the station with his tie in one hand and his briefcase in the other."

Sometimes when he returned at 4:00 AM from a political meeting he would wake Erna from a deep sleep, in order to work on a price list for another building job that he would need that morning at work.

Janis's strong support of his country and community was so time consuming that Pauline would at times complain that there was not enough time for him to plan and build their own dream house.

When she complained he would ask her, "Is there anything in life that you need, that you lack?"

She would admit that she had everything that she needed, which included a closet full of her much loved shoes. Janis insisted that they buy only good jewelry. Erna was not allowed to wear any cheap or gaudy jewelry, "like the gypsies". One time she bought a large inexpensive, decorative pin that was set with colorful artificial gems. She thought that the pin was pretty and it made her happy to wear it. When she wore the pin to dinner one evening her father was not impressed with her "gypsy jewelry".

Erna, Zigfrids and Pauline

"Then you must understand that if your family's needs are met and you have money you are to help others in need." he emphatically exclaimed.

Erna learned the relevance of that lesson when her best friend, Elza, did not have a dress for their confirmation. Elza's father, a financially struggling tailor, could not afford to buy her a confirmation dress. Janis readily provided the money for Elza's dress so that she and Erna could go through confirmation together.

An example of Janis's generosity to the community was when he built a new community center for Ligatne. When it was finished the town presented him with an engraved watch to thank him for his service. Years later, when they were reunited, Erna gave this watch to her brother, Zigfrids.

On one occasion their factory caught fire and a portion of it burned down. Even though there was a pond nearby they had no way to pump the water to put out the fire. Janis organized a volunteer fire department and purchased a fire truck that could pump the water from the pond. This consequently saved many buildings and homes in the village from being destroyed by fire.

5.

1932-1933

Into The World

Leaving Home

THE WORLD CAME to Ligatne when Janis purchased a radio in 1932. Real time happenings from afar were brought into their kitchen, as the many workers and townspeople gathered with Janis and his family, around their kitchen table, to listen to the world news. As this world came into their home, it was time for Erna to leave.

1932 was the year that Erna left home to go to Volola Academy. The school was in Riga, too far away for her to come home every night. Aunt Anna, who used to bring her colored pencils and paper dolls and sew pretty dresses for her when she was little, still lived in Riga. She was delighted to have her niece stay with her while she attended business school. Of course that arrangement was also very agreeable to Erna, who adored her aunt.

The students at the business school were required to wear uniforms. The girls wore green wool dresses with white collars in the winter, and green cotton skirts with white blouses in the summer. Both uniforms were accessorized with polished black shoes on their feet, and on their head, a black beret, decorated with a green ribbon embroidered with the school's initials. It was mandatory that they wear the beret whenever they were outside of the school, especially while walking in the city. Everyday their uniforms were inspected by the head mistress. There could be no wrinkles or spots of any kind and the shoes had to be freshly polished. Luckily, Aunt Anna, who was a seamstress, made Erna several uniforms so that she didn't have to launder and press them every night. By the time that she had finished school she recalled that she was definitely sick of the color green.

Even though her father gave her money to ride the trolley to and from school, Erna preferred to walk because she would pass by the music school on her way to the academy. She would save up the trolley fare and then take her best friend to a restaurant for a treat; peas with ham and buttermilk to drink.

Every morning she would leave her aunt's early enough to allow her an extra ten minutes, in order to have time to stop by the music school. She would stand outside of the conservatory and listen wistfully to the students as they played piano.

Erna's love for piano had begun when she was in elementary school. There was a teacher who had a piano. Sometimes when Erna was running errands for her mother she would go by the teacher's house and stop for a moment to listen to her playing.

This teacher noticed Erna as she stood and listened, and invited her to come in, asking her, "Would you like to try to play the piano?"

Erna enthusiastically replied, "Yes!"

"Well then, come in and you can try, but first you must go and wash your hands," The teacher instructed. From that moment on Erna was hooked.

Although she had given up her dream to be a piano teacher she still was able to continue her piano lessons at her aunt's house. Erna's father understood her love for music and told her to keep it in her heart. She loved playing the piano, despite that one particularly mean teacher who sat beside Erna with a ruler clasped in her hand, ready to smack those fingers if they hit a wrong note.

When she complained about it to her father he told her, "Just put up with it. The teacher just wants you to play well."

The business school required the students to learn German and English. To pass those language classes, the student would be expected to translate a story written in Latvian into English and German. Erna did not like learning German and struggled with it, so Janis hired her teacher to tutor her after class. After awhile, she decided to study a little harder, so that she would not have to be tutored "by that grouchy old man" and would instead have that hour for ice skating. She preferred learning English, but eventually came to realize how knowing those two languages helped her survive during the war.

Chemistry and physics were also subjects that she found very challenging, and for the most part remembered working very hard for those four years. She recalled often thinking that she did not know what she would do if she flunked any of her classes, realizing how disappointed her father would be.

At the business school there were no frills, no parties or dances. Between classes they were given 10 minutes to walk around the school for exercise. On the two days a week that Erna did not have piano lessons after school, she was able to ice skate. At the rink there was a place to change with a locker for her school uniform. She would change into her ice skating skirt there.

Back at her aunt's, in the evening, she would play bingo with her younger cousin. Aunt Anna was a seamstress and would sometimes use that evening time to teach Erna how to make button holes.

When Janis was in Riga on business he would visit her at her aunt's, often bringing Erna and her cousin gifts. While there he would also stop by the school in order to check up on her progress. It seemed that her father was everywhere, always keeping track of his daughter.

One time a young man in Erna's class asked her to help him write a heading on his paper using calligraphy, since she was very good at it. He promised, "I will carry your books and walk you back to your aunt's apartment if you will help me with this header."

Erna agreed, but didn't realize that her father was in town, and had observed her walking with the young man. After they arrived at Aunt Anna's, she wrote the header for him, he thanked her, and then left.

Shortly after he had left, Janis showed up at the apartment. "I saw you walking home with a young man. Who is he?"

She explained, "Just a classmate that wanted my help with a paper."

Her father replied, "He looks Italian and if he is Italian he is Catholic." In Latvia at that time there was a strict separation between Catholics and Lutherans, they did not mix socially.

Erna admitted that she used to ask her daughters when they were dating someone new, "Is he Catholic?" " I had to make myself stop doing that. It was just something that had been instilled in me at a young age."

Summer Breaks

During the summers, before their internships began, there was a short break where the students could go home and visit their families. On one of those breaks Erna arrived home, walked into the living room, and discovered a beautiful new piano standing there. She had often dreamed of having her own piano, but it never occurred to her to ask her father to buy one for her. When she saw that piano she could not believe her eyes and started to cry.

"I didn't buy you a piano to make you cry," A bewildered Janis said, "I thought that it would make you happy."

"I am crying because I am happy!" she replied through her tears.

Erna spent three consecutive summers serving the internships that were included in her school curriculum. She was not permitted to intern in her own father's business, so the first summer she was assigned to a business in Sigulda, where she worked as a bookkeeper. One of the advantages of working in Sigulda was that she could live at home in Ligatne. However, Erna had to peddle her bicycle for one hour to go to work and then again for one hour, at the end of the day, to return home. If the weather was bad she stayed overnight with the store manager's family.

Her second year's internship was served as a cashier in a warehouse outside Riga. During that time she boarded with a family who lived near the warehouse. One of her responsibilities was to take the cash from each day's business transactions to the train station and give the money to the conductor, who, in turn, delivered it to the bank employee in Riga, who would deposit it.

Her third internship was as a cashier, at a warehouse, once again, in Sigulda. Happily, this enabled her to stay at her parents' home; but it also necessitated the resumption of her bicycle commute, since there was no reliable train service available between Sigulda and Ligatne, due to erratic train schedules.

At the end of each summer internship, Erna would return in the fall to the business school. The school routines were the same throughout the remaining years as the students continued a rigorous course of study in pursuit of their ultimate goal of earning a Certificate of Achievement in each class, which would allow them to be graduated from this prestigious school.

Volola Academy in Riga

6.

1936-1938

Achievement And Passages

Graduation

WHEN THE FINAL YEAR of business school ended there were exams in each subject to take. On their last day, after the exams, they lined up in the auditorium, not knowing if they had passed or failed. The teachers were seated behind a long table. One at a time the students would go to each of their teachers and if they passed their class they would receive a certificate. If they didn't pass they would get a handshake and a "better luck next time." Erna learned, with great relief, that she had passed all of her classes and would graduate. During the school years there were no dances, no dates, no boyfriends or girlfriends; but after graduation there was a graduation ball in the auditorium for their celebration.

Bursting with excitement Erna literally ran to the train station and boarded the first train that would take her home. As her train pulled

into the station in Ligatne, she
looked out of her window and
saw her father anxiously waiting
for her on the platform. His one
question to her as she exited the
train was "Did you pass?"

Waving her diploma she answered,
"I did!"

*Back row, third from the left - Erna,
with classmates and teacher*

"Oh, I am so proud of you!" he exclaimed.

At last Janis had the helper he needed in his business. That he had
the same hopes and expectations for Erna that a father often has for a son
seemed especially unusual for that time period.

When they arrived home Janis told Erna, "Now that you have your diploma it is time that you study for your confirmation in the Lutheran Church."

Lutheran Church in Sigulda

Erna's Confirmation

For the next two weeks she traveled by train everyday to the Lutheran Church in Sigulda where she studied for her confirmation. On
the day that she was confirmed she invited many of her friends to attend

the ceremony. Afterwards, as she left the church, her friends handed her fragrant bouquets of flowers. Her friends and family were invited to a celebration dinner in her honor. Everyone enjoyed the delicious food and Erna received many gifts. Her parents gave her a gold watch with four diamonds as a graduation and confirmation gift, a gift that became much more valuable to Erna several years later.

The Family Business

With graduation and confirmation behind her, Erna began working in her father's business. She worked with the book keeper for two weeks in order to learn his job since he would be retiring soon and she would replace him. It was very important that the books were kept accurately in case the tax department dropped in, unannounced, to audit their accounts. This was an arduous task since Janis's business had expanded considerably. He was building schools, hospitals and post offices all over Latvia. Many of these buildings are still standing today. It was an immense amount of responsibility for a young woman.

Her father told her, "You are to arrive at work at 8:00 AM. You must never be late. It is important that you set an example for the other workers. You must understand that if you want anything in life you must work very hard for it."

Janis Construction Project

Erna in front of her father's Ligatne factory in 2010

Romance and Marriage

Erna's Gypsy pin.

In the fall of 1936, Erna was in her office carefully going over the accounts for her father's business. A handsome young man with dark curly hair, having just delivered a load of lumber from his father's saw mill, came into her office and introduced himself. His name was Arijs Freimanis. He had noticed Erna measuring the lumber when he delivered it and was a little surprised to see her doing that. Erna was very excited since he was really good looking and she had not had much of an opportunity for dating.

After their initial introduction, whenever he brought lumber to the factory, he would drop in her office to say hello. Eventually he found the courage to ask her if she would like to go with him to visit his family, who lived on a farm out in the country. Her father enthusiastically approved because he knew Arijs's father through their businesses. He also thought that maybe having a boyfriend would help to settle his daughter down, since he knew that she was still dreaming about a career in music, not business.

On the following Sunday Arijs came to pick Erna up in a horse and buggy. They rode to his family's home in the country, where his mother had prepared a delicious meal for them. After they had eaten, they

Arijs' parents, Janis and Julija Freimanis

spent the rest of the day playing games. Erna had a wonderful time and returned home all excited, because now she had a boyfriend.

Laipni lūdzam Jūs pagodināt ar savu klātbūtni

mūsu laulības

1937. g. 23. oktobrī pulkst. 18³⁰ Araišu baznīcā, un pēc
tam kāzu viesībās Rāmulu pag., Lejas-Klauslēs

Erna Mūrmanis

Arijs Freimanis

Lūdzam minētā dienā pulkst. 17⁰⁰ ierasties Līgatnē, Mūrmaņa mājās.

Wedding Invitation

Their relationship quickly
grew serious and they set a wedding date for October of the
next year. They were married on
October 23, 1937 in the beautiful
Araisu Church. The ceremony was
small and quiet, although many
of her school mates came bringing her flowers and good wishes.
On the following day they were
honored at a reception in her husband's home. The day after that,
her family hosted a reception for
them at their house.

Bridal Portrait

Part Two

7.

1939-1940

Disruption And Occupation

AFTER THE WEDDING Erna and Arijs continued to work in her father's business until Arijs had to leave for his mandatory service in the Latvian air force. They had moved into her parent's home where they were given their own rooms. Her brother, Zigfrids, was attending a private trade school at the time, studying to be an architect. Like his sister, Zigfrids had had other dreams. He had wanted to be a sailor, just as she had hoped to teach piano, but their father needed and expected them to work in his business.

Erna had hoped that she and Arijs might eventually live in the apartment that was above the new factory in Sigulda. Perhaps when her brother finished his training he would work in the factory near their home in Ligatne and she could run the new factory.

Unfortunately, the events of the world would soon disrupt their lives and plans. In 1939 the Latvian people started to think and worry a bit more about the war. During that year the Germans, who lived in Latvia, began leaving. They tried to persuade Janis to move to Germany.

He refused, saying, "We are Latvian and we are going to be all right."

Arijs and Erna Freimanis - 1939

Janis was not aware that a secret pact, The Nazi-Soviet Non Aggression Pact, also known as The Molotov-Ribbentrop Pact had been signed on August 23, 1939 by the Soviet Union and Nazi Germany. This pact essentially gave Latvia, Estonia, and eventually Lithuania to the Soviet Union. On October 5, 1939 the Soviet Union forced Latvia into signing the Pact of Defense and Mutual Assistance and to accept the occupation of 30,000 Soviet troops. This number was increased by 100,000 troops on June 17, 1940. (History of Latvia, A Brief Summary p.33)

On that day in June, Erna was in Riga on business. As she tried to reach the train station to return home, thousands of soldiers, tanks, and trucks were clogging the streets. The air was filled with Russian voices shouting orders over the roar of the tank and truck engines. She remembered that her father had often said that Russia always had its eye on Latvia because of its Baltic Sea coastline where the water never froze, making it important for shipping. As she struggled to cross the street to board the train, she realized that life was not going to be the same. She told herself to forget about the good things and think about what will be tomorrow.

Finally she was able to board the train and return home. Her mother was waiting for her and informed her "We do not have Latvia anymore. The Russians have invaded."

Just as a thief had taken everything that they owned when they returned to Latvia almost 20 years ago; on this day the Russians had taken everything; their business, their bank accounts, and their country from them. Their loss was much greater this time, but Janis still found gratitude in having his family.

Baby

Erna didn't know what to do or think. She was pregnant with her first child. Her husband had been away serving his mandatory time in the Latvian Airforce . She had no idea where he was because when the Russians took over Latvia the Latvian servicemen were immediately released from service. They had to go into hiding to avoid being picked up and transported to Siberia, imprisoned, or even shot by the Russians. One never knew what person would be taken away. Arijs hid, afraid that they might arrest him. Janis was away from their home in Ligatne, building schools and hospitals. Consequently, Erna and Pauline were not sure how to locate him. They could not imagine what the morning would bring.

What it eventually brought were Russian officers into their home. The officers informed them that for the time being they could stay in their house. The Soviets had already taken over Janis's business and bank accounts, even his car keys and motorcycle. He was told that he was to continue working on his building contracts, but now he would be working for the Soviet government.

Cesis Bank

Erna was informed that as soon as she delivered her baby she was to go to work for a bank in Cesis and was no longer allowed to work in what was once her father's business. She was allowed to go to her office and retrieve her belongings. On entering her old office to clear out her desk, she was surprised to see that a former factory worker, an employee of her father, had been put in charge of running the factory and had been assigned her office. She had no idea that he had become a communist.

August arrived and so did Erna's approaching due date. Her parents made arrangements for her to stay with Aunt Anna for a few days before the baby was due. Luckily, Arijs was able to get to the hospital in time and on August 18, 1940, at 8:00 P.M. Astride was born.

Janis looked at his beautiful new granddaughter and said for the second time in his life, "Girl, I have lost everything that I had in my life but I have my granddaughter."

Janis, with his dog Rixsis, and baby Astride on a blanket

Pauline and Astride

Shortly after she gave birth to Astride, Erna had to go to work in the bank in Cesis. The Russians provided day care for their workers, but Pauline would not allow her to take Astride with her to Cesis and have her granddaughter put in Russian day care. Pauline insisted that Astride would stay with her during the week, where she could sleep in her handsome new crib that had been constructed, especially for her, at her grandfather's furniture factory.

Erna would return to Ligatne to be with her baby on the weekends. Arijs went to stay with his parents in a wooded area in the country, near Cesis, thinking that he would be safer there. This was how they lived for the next year, known in Latvian's history as the "Year of Terror."

Erna pushing baby Astride in a sled

Erna holding baby Astride

8.

1941

Time Of Terror

DURING THE NIGHT on June 14, 1941, one year after the beginning of the Russian occupation of Latvia, Janis heard a knock on his bedroom window. Cautiously, he opened the window. As his eyes adjusted to the darkness, he recognized a familiar face, a former employee who had become an active member of the Communist party. The worker, who remembered Janis's previous generosity and kindness towards him and his large family, risked his life to warn his former employer, "You must leave the house immediately. Do not ask any questions."

Janis did not hesitate. He left his home and family and went to his foreman's apartment where he asked the foreman to take him to the countryside. From there he escaped into the woods, where he hid. The forest around the Ligatne-Cesis area provided tenuous safety for anti Soviet groups and individuals who sought shelter under the many trees, often depending upon the sympathetic farmers in the area for food.

At 7:00 A.M. that same morning Russian officers came to Pauline and Janis's house. Pauline, Zigfrids (age 16), the grandfather, and baby

Astride were still there. The officers ordered Pauline to put the belongings that they wanted to take with them in a pillow case. As she packed their warm clothing, she tucked her valuable jewelry inside of the pockets, out of sight. This jewelry, that Janis insisted that she have, helped keep them alive during their years in Siberia. The valuable jewelry bought them food and some small favors such as an extra blanket for warmth. Ironically, along with the valuable jewelry, Pauline had included the inexpensive, colorful pin that Erna had bought years before. Pauline kept that pin with her during her years in Siberia and gave the pin to Astride when she was finally released and reunited with her family.

The officers herded them into a truck that was waiting in front of their house. Astride was left in the house, in her play pen. It is impossible to imagine what Pauline was thinking when she was forced to leave her granddaughter there. Was it perhaps relief, since it was unlikely that an infant would survive in Siberia? Or relief that they did not kill Astride right then? Perhaps Pauline was able to pull her maid aside and quietly tell her to call Erna.

Apparently they did not take Astride because she was considered to be in "another family", Arijs's family. Even though she was not even a year old that event was imprinted in Astride's memory.

She said that even today she could still recall a mental picture of those officers in their uniforms coming into their room and taking her grandmother, great grandfather and uncle away.

June 14, 1941 is known to Latvians as "The Black Day" when over 15,000 Latvians were deported in cattle cars to Siberia. The deportees were Latvia's elite; the businessmen, scientists, teachers, politicians, army officers, all of the highly educated. Those are the people that an occupying power does not want to deal with because they are literate, they are leaders and they ask questions. Over 35,000 Latvians were exiled to Siberia or executed during this occupation. The exportation included over 5000 women and over 3000 children. (The Library of Congress Studies, Latvia Independence 1918-1940, p. 6) Of course Janis was the one that the officers really wanted but since he was not there they took his family, hoping to get information from them as to where he might be hiding.

Erna was working at the bank in Cesis that morning when she received a call from one of the girls who worked for her mother. Fighting back hysteria, she told Erna, "The Russians have taken your mother, grandfather, and brother! They have left Astride all alone in her playpen! You must come and get your daughter!"

The bank manager saw that Erna was extremely upset and asked her what was wrong.

"My baby is left alone; they have taken my mother, brother and grandfather. I need to go back home to get her." She replied, trying not to panic.

"No, don't you go anyplace. I will make arrangements. I will bring your daughter to you." He promised.

The bank manager, a Russian officer, called the maid and told her "Get all of the baby's belongings together and bring her to Cesis on the train. I am coming to get her."

Erna was numb. She spent the day praying and waiting. At sunset the bank manager brought Astride to her and she thought "they have taken my mother, brother, and grandfather. I don't know where my father is. But at least I got my girl back."

As she held Astride tightly in her arms, she asked the bank officer, "Where is my family? What is happening?"

"They are in a boxcar, on their way to Siberia. I will try to arrange a visit for you. Get food and warm blankets for them. We will catch their train when it comes near the station."

A foreman from her father's factory took her by motorcycle to meet the train. She had been given a permission slip which allowed her fifteen minutes to see her mother, brother and grandfather. Erna brought blankets, cheese and cold meat. At the station the train stopped. The soldiers opened the door to the box car. There was her mother standing near the doorway.

"Don't cry. It will be alright. Take care of your little girl."

Her brother, Zigfrids, stood there waving to her. He kept saying, "Don't cry. Don't cry. We will see you soon." She saw her grandfather sitting on the floor. Then the soldiers closed the door.

A few days later a letter addressed to Erna was brought to her. Someone had found it alongside of the train tracks. Her brother had tossed the letter from the train as it pulled away and miraculously it found its way to her. The letter said, "We are headed to nowhere. Good bye."

Erna's Uncle Peteris, Pauline's younger brother, went into the woods and hanged himself when he found out what had happened to his sister. He was grief stricken that his family had been taken to Siberia, where his father would die.

The bank manager had saved Erna from Siberia by arranging for the maid to bring Astride to Cesis. If Erna had gone back to get Astride she too would have been deported. Her baby would have been the bait. It was rumored that this bank manager had a little girl back in Russia who he had not seen for four years. Perhaps that is why he risked his own life to help Erna reunite with Astride.

Janis remained in hiding for several months. Arijs, her husband, was also hiding. Erna had no idea where they were and felt abandoned and utterly alone without any of her family. Shortly after her family was taken to Siberia, Russian officers took Erna to jail. For an entire day, they interrogated her about her father. She kept telling them that she had no idea where he was and that she needed to go home to her baby.

She kept repeating, "I don't know where he is. I didn't live there. I have a little girl at home."

Finally they released her. There were posters all over Riga offering rewards of 10,000 lats to anyone who could provide information as to where Janis was hiding. Besides being a successful businessman, he had also been very active in politics and had often spoken against the Soviet occupation. If they had found him he would have been shot. Erna said that she was under constant surveillance; always being watched for any indication that she was in contact with her father.

She lived in continual fear for her life. The Latvians were often gunned down in the streets if they were at all suspected of having any connections to the Soviet's enemies. One day as she walked home from the bank she noticed a 14 year old boy walking in front of her. She was also aware that a Russian soldier was walking behind her. Suddenly there were loud gun shots and the boy fell to the ground in front of her. Erna said that all she could do was look straight ahead and keep walking, while inside she shook from terror and shock.

Another time, in the early morning darkness, while her father was still in hiding, a stranger knocked on Erna's door.

Without any explanation he handed her a basket and instructed her "Fill this with food and any warm clothing that you can find."
The stranger worked at a stable in the country where the horses that were used in the city were cared for and kept. Every morning he would

bring the horses to the city and then would come back for them in the evening.

Erna could not find any more warm clothing but was able to fill the basket with meat and cheese. That evening the stranger returned to retrieve the basket. Not a word was spoken between them, yet Erna realized that this food was going to her father, who was spending his time in hiding, going from farm to farm. He relied on the support of the people that he knew, but this was done at great risk because there was no way to know which farmers had turned communist.

Germany Invades Latvia

Then in July, 1941, Nazi Germany's armed forces invaded Latvia, driving out the Russians. One July evening there was a knock at Erna's door. Cautiously, she opened the door and there stood her father, dirty and unshaven. Erna was overwhelmed with relief and joy since now she at least had her father back. She had no idea how Janis had found her. She fed him. He then cleaned up and immediately returned to Ligatne. With the Russians gone it was safe for him to come out of hiding.

The Germans took over Latvia, and for Erna, her father and many native Latvians, life was a little bit better. Unfortunately for many others; the Jews, the gypsies, the Latvians who had cooperated with the Russians, life was much worse. They were shot or sent to concentration camps by the thousands. It is estimated that the Nazis exterminated around 90,000 Latvian Jews and gypsies.

After the Germans took over, Erna would often look at the coin that the Russian Bank manager had given her to remember him, when he fled Latvia before the Nazis arrived. She would always keep him in her prayers, and hoped for his safe return to his family.

The German's presence in Latvia was also a frightening time. One morning, on her way to work, Erna observed deep trenches being dug. She called one of her relatives who was in the police department and asked him, "What is happening? There are men here digging a deep trench."

"You don't want to know" he told her, "Just get to work as quickly as possible."

Later that day she learned that the people who had been digging the trench were forced to line up facing it. As the Germans shot them they would fall face first into the trench, which was then hurriedly covered up to become a mass grave. On her way home from work that day she noticed that there was no longer any trench, the ground was perfectly level. Many years later when Erna returned to Latvia she remembered exactly where that mass grave was.

9.

1942-1943

Borrowed Time

A Return To The Factory And Family Life

IN COMPARISON TO THE RUSSIANS, many Latvians and Estonians
felt that they were treated better by the Germans. Erna's ability to speak
German, a language that she hated to learn as a student, also helped
her to survive. The Germans allowed Janis to run his business again,
although they retained ownership and did not return his property to him.
Erna, Arijs and Janis worked full time in their former factories under the
Germans. Arijs and Erna rented a small house in Cesis, where Arijs's
mother, who was in poor health, came to live with them for awhile. Janis
was able to reoccupy the family home in Ligatne and in 1942 he invited
Erna and Arijs to come live with him, since Erna was expecting her
second child.

Three year old Astride would often accompany her mother to work in her grandfather's former factory. There was a certain employee under Erna's charge who had a problem with drinking, often showing up late to work. Erna tried to cover for him but the commandant eventually noticed and told Erna (in front of Astride). "If he comes in late again you will fire him."

Erna knew that she would have to have the talk with this worker. Before he left work that evening she called him aside, "You must not come to work late again or I will have to let you go."

"Don't worry," he replied, "Astride has already told me."

As she remembered incidents such as this, Erna realized, sadly, that Astride never had a real childhood, she was a little girl with an old soul.

Astride Solveiga Freimanis

On May 13, 1943, Erna delivered her second daughter, Rudite Vija in the hospital nearest to them in Cesis. Then, after Christmas in 1943, Erna and Arijs moved to Sigulda to operate the factory there. They brought with them the maid, Pauline Varna, from Janis's home, to help them. Also, Erna hired a nanny, Vilma, to help with the small children while she and her husband worked at the factory.

Astride, during this stressful time, had started pulling out her hair in one spot. Sadly, Erna had to cut her daughter's long thick braids to try to get her to stop. Shortly after the haircut, Astride began to have severe stomach pains. Frantically, Erna flagged down a German delivery truck at her work that was traveling to Riga. She begged the driver to give her a ride to the hospital, explaining that it was an emergency and she needed to get her daughter there.

At the hospital it was determined that Astride was having an appendicitis attack and she was rushed into surgery. To everyone's surprise, when the doctor operated on Astride, he discovered that it wasn't her appendix, but instead a large ball of hair in her stomach that had caused the pain.

Exhausted, Erna returned home and ironically began to have stomach pains herself. Once again she asked the daily delivery truck driver to take her back to the hospital, where she had an emergency appendectomy. As she woke up from the surgery she recalled seeing Astride's sweet little face looking at her from the adjacent bed. The nurses had arranged to keep Astride in the hospital until Erna was well enough to go home also.

Erna and Astride

10.

1944

Leaving Latvia

Preparing For Travel

EARLY IN THE SUMMER of 1944, Janis was again warned that the Russians would be returning. Some of the Germans were fleeing Latvia and offered him transportation to the Port Liepaja. Once again he refused to leave Latvia saying, "No, everything will be alright."

By mid July of 1944 the Russians had defeated the Germans on the eastern front and were entering Latvia's prewar eastern border. On August 18, 1944, Astride's fourth birthday, they could hear the artillery and bombs exploding near Cesis.

"Oh no, they must be coming! Get a few things together and be ready to go," Janis directed Erna. He had often told her to be ready in case they had to leave in a hurry.

In anticipation of this hurried departure he had prepared a horse drawn wagon with a special platform. Fortunately, they still had Grandfather's horse. Amazingly the Russians had not taken the horse from them the first time that they invaded. Erna didn't know what to do. She told Astride, "Grandfather is coming soon and we are going for a ride."

Little four year old Astride kept asking, "Why? Why?"

Erna packed a little back pack with Astride's and 16 month old Rudite's clothing and Astride's teddy bear. She packed another suitcase for Arijs and herself and brought blankets and coats. She then went to the hospital to get her husband discharged. He couldn't walk due to a back injury and had been placed in the hospital.

At first he refused to go, afraid that he would be a burden for them. "I am not coming," he said. "go on without me."

Erna returned home and told her father that Arijs wouldn't come.

The maid, Vilma, who had been in an orphanage before she came to work for Erna's mother said, "I am going to come with you, if you will take me."

While they were preparing to leave they received a message from Arijs. He had changed his mind and decided to go with them. They returned to the hospital to get him.

As they set out in the wagon on their journey, Astride, with her braids bouncing needed to see everything, so she sat beside her grandfather, as he held the reins. She was like a little soldier, never once complaining or shedding a tear, just constantly chattering away to Janis. Arijs was lying in the wagon while Erna walked. At times Janis would jump down and walk for awhile, allowing her to ride. She knew that she had to be strong and not fall apart, especially since she was four months pregnant and would never be able to see a doctor throughout the pregnancy. In preparation for the trip she had visited her doctor who was one of the most respected doctors in Latvia. He offered her some advice since he had raised children during war and also gave her drops to put in her children's hair to help prevent lice.

Erna - 1944

Leipaja

Another passenger on their trip was Janis's little black hound, Rixsis. Besides being an astute businessman, Janis was a great marksman and won all of the skeet shooting contests at the Ligatne Hunter's club. He especially loved to hunt rabbits with his faithful companion, Rixsis. He and Rixsis were inseparable. Perched on Janis's motorcycle, the little dog would ride all over town with his master. That he would leave Rixsis behind on this trip was out of the question. As Janis drove the wagon, the little hound would normally sit very patiently beside him. Unfortunately, one day, as they were riding along, Rixsis unexpectedly jumped from the wagon and was immediately run over by a German car. Erna would never forget her heart broken father digging a grave for his little friend at the side of the road.

They traveled on to an aunt's house, which was on the way to Riga, where they stayed the first night. There they were able to wash and get something warm to eat. The aunt provided food, especially lots of apples, to take on the journey. Janis left some of his wife's possessions at the aunt's house to save for her, just in case she was able to return to Latvia.

Early the next morning they made their way to Riga where they needed to cross a bridge to get to the port on the coast of Latvia. They could hear the bombing getting closer and knew that at anytime Riga would fall.

A soldier, who was a previous employee, told them "Hurry and get across. The German Army is going to blow up the bridge anytime now."

With bombs exploding all around them, they made it safely across the bridge.

They traveled early in the morning and afternoon, finding it safer to travel in daylight when they could see the road and what was ahead of them. It was not unusual for them to come across the bodies of people and horses lying in the road, having been hit by the machine guns from the low flying aircraft, which constantly flew over them, as they tried to escape.

Riga in 2012

When the horse needed a rest they would look for a shady place to stop. In the evening they would seek shelter in the forest, or they might find a farmer's barn where they could have a roof over their heads and a soft bed in the hay for the night. Often the farmers would help them, especially when they saw the two beautiful little girls. Erna described her daughters as "little angels, never crying or fussing. No mother could ask for better children." There would often be some milk offered to the children and maybe some bread. She said, "That bread was like gold."

She does not remember what she ate, if anything, but would always try to tuck some of the bread away to give to her daughters as they traveled. It seemed miraculous to Erna that the infant in her womb survived with such little nourishment. "She must have been God's child," she declared.

When they were at times offered a place to wash, it was a wonderful bonus.

Eventually they arrived at Arijs' cousin's, who took care of a manor. This was a luxurious stop. They had baths, a warm meal (instead of just bread, milk and cheese) and a warm place to sleep for one night. Cousin Milda provided Arijs with some comfort from his pain, by providing him with some white pills prescribed by a nearby German officer, who was a doctor.

At this point, they were half way to the port. Janis hoped that when they finally arrived at the port that there would still be ships. Sometimes it rained and they would find shelter under the trees or under the tarps on the wagon. When there were air raids they would stop and seek protection in the forest. Luckily, the bombs never hit them. Throughout all of this, pregnant Erna was caring for two babies and an invalid husband.

After traveling for over a month, at last, one evening in early October, they arrived at the Port Liepaja. They stopped in a park that was packed with refugees waiting to get on a ship. While the adults were getting their wagon and horse situated and surveying the area, four year old Astride ("my little busy body daughter") slipped off of the wagon. No one noticed that she was gone until she came back holding the hand of an elderly gentleman. When they saw her, Erna and Janis were surprised and worried, since one had to be very careful who they talked to in case they were communist spies.

Astride announced to them, (as if she was 40 instead of 4) "Grandfather, this man wants to talk to you."

The gentleman informed them "Two ships will sail tomorrow in the evening. You need to be here very early in the morning."

This kind stranger took them back to his home where Erna had the opportunity to straighten out their clothing, bathe the children and wash their hair. Since Astride refused to have her long braids cut, keeping her hair clean was very difficult. Regardless of the circumstances, Erna took pride in always keeping her children as clean as possible.

Janis went back to the port for more information and to pay for their passage. When he returned he instructed Erna, "Get ready to leave early in the morning."

Each passenger was allowed one suitcase. Astride was ready with her back pack with the children's clothing and her teddy bear. At least for that night they had a warm meal and a place to sleep while they waited to see what the morning would bring.

Before dawn the next morning they climbed into the wagon and returned to the port. There were only two ships docked 100 feet apart, waiting to leave. The area near the ships was crowded to overflowing with Latvians hoping to gain passage. Janis registered and checked in his family. He then gave the horse, wagon and most of their possessions to the kind gentleman who had helped them. Once again, they had nothing except a few necessities. Their lives were contained in one suitcase.

The soldiers were allowed on the ship first. As Erna and the remaining passengers crowded on the ship she prayed, "God keep us safe."

There was standing room only, but luckily Arijs was now able to stand due to the pills that cousin Milda had given him. The passengers stood pressed person to person, unable to move. When it was dark, at 7:00 or 8:00 P.M., the ship began to leave port. Suddenly the sound of sirens pierced the darkness and the bombing began. The ship that was docked beside them in port was hit, burst into flames and began to sink into the black waters, taking its passengers with it. Most of them were lost in the dark turbulent sea. Watching in horror, Erna could not help but think how lucky she and her family were to not have been on that ship. Astride, to this day, can still remember the port being bombed and the ship and market area exploding.

The survivors from the bombed ship joined the passengers on Erna's ship, which made it even more crowded. Erna has often wondered how she ever survived that trip. There was very little food. Celery, grapefruit and occasionally a sandwich were passed around to the passengers. Since she was pregnant the smell of the celery made her extremely ill. Today the sight and smell of celery still brings back the memory of that nausea. Erna remembered four year old Astride, looking hungrily at a sandwich, and then saying, "No, mama, give the sandwich to Rudite. She is sick."

The children rested on the floor of the ship. There was a bench where Erna could occasionally lie down. Luckily her little girls were toilet trained and never once had an accident. She would take one of them to the ship's head while the Polish girl watched the other one.

"I was so scared and worried that I felt numb like a mummy. I looked at my little girls and wondered, 'What will happen to you?'"That is how Erna described how she felt throughout the ordeal.

They left Latvia during the second week of October and after two long weeks on the ship they docked in Poland. Throughout their time on the ship Erna described her little girls as "little angels who never cried or whined." Somehow, as their mother, she was able to convey a sense of calmness and security to her children that she herself did not really feel.

From the ship they were taken in German trucks to a bath house where they showered and were disinfected. While she and her daughters waited in line at the bath house they could see another line of women and children wearing what seemed to be burlap bags with an opening for their heads. They could hear them sobbing and saw the children clinging to their mothers. Erna wondered if she and her children were going to have to wear those bags also. She was told that those women and children were Jewish and were going to be taken to Auschwitz. German doctors and nurses checked Erna and her family over. Janis and the girl who had worked for them were taken by the Germans for forced labor. They did not take Arijs since he could not work due to his back injury.

Janis reassured his daughter, "Don't worry. After war I will find you." He walked away carrying his briefcase. Erna's mother, grandfather and brother had already been taken from her. At that moment, she had no idea what would happen to her father and where he would be.

Erna was left with an invalid husband, two little girls, and another baby on the way. Her little girls clung to her during their long wait, never once crying, just looking around. After what seemed like many hours had passed they were taken, standing like cattle, in the back of another German truck, to the railroad station and put on a train which was headed to Pottersdam, Czechoslovakia.

Czechoslovakia

It seemed as though she was on the train for months. The refugees were given one meal a day. Whenever the train made a stop the Red Cross and the Salvation Army would be waiting by the tracks, ready to hand the refugees care packages of food, and provide milk for the children. They would also check on the children to see if they needed medical help. As she rode on the train Erna would look out the windows. As they passed through the towns she would stare at the houses that flashed by, wondering when she would live in a house again.

It was like that through November, passing through town after town. Rudite began to run a high fever and there was no medicine for her. Erna was sick with worry, not knowing what to do.

Finally, in desperation, at one stop, Erna approached the German commander in charge of the train and spoke to him in German, "My baby is running a very high fever and I don't know what I can do. She needs medicine!"

The commander reassured her, "Don't worry. I will notify the Red Cross. They will find a doctor."

The doctor came on the train, examined Rudite and then warned Erna, "She will not survive if we don't put her in the hospital."

Erna felt that her heart was breaking. She didn't know what to do, or what would happen to her little girl.

Two nuns came to the train to get the sick child. The nuns reassured Erna, "We will take good care of her. She will get better. Don't worry."

With great trepidation she placed her child in the out stretched arms of the nun; there was nothing else to do since Rudite was so ill. Erna had to put her trust in complete strangers, not knowing if she would ever see her little girl again. And how could she explain to a child so young why she was being given to these strangers?

Two weeks later Erna received a message that her daughter was getting better. She hoped that they would be reunited once she was settled in a refugee camp. She recalled how much she had hated to learn German when she went to business school and yet being able to communicate in German with the commander, doctor, and the nuns definitely helped to save little Rudite's life.

There were two sisters and their mother traveling with Erna. One of the girl's husbands had been conscripted by the German army and the other sister did not know where her husband was. They helped Erna with her children and reassured her about Rudite. While the war continued around them.

During the heaviest bombing the train would go into underground tunnels and wait until the bombing was over. At the end of November the train at last arrived in Pottersdam, Czechoslovakia. The refugees were given a place to stay in an abandoned school. Erna and her family shared one room with at least four other families. Each family was given a set of bunk beds, which provided no privacy. The bathrooms were in the hall. There was no way for them to cook, but food was brought to them each day. Soup was ladled out with some bread and they ate it or went without. In the basement there were sinks with hot water and laundry tubs where they could wash themselves, wash their clothes, and bathe the children. Each family was given a specific time when they could do their laundry. Erna's time was 2:00 A.M.. Since she could not leave her daughter alone, and Arijs refused to take any responsibility for her care, the sisters would stay with Astride while Erna was doing her laundry.

Shortly after their arrival in Pottersdam, there was good news. Rudite was better. The two sisters offered to go to the hospital and bring her back to her mother. " We will go and get Rudite. You need to stay here with Astride. It is not a good time for you to risk traveling, since you are due to have your baby soon."

Reluctantly, Erna agreed. The sisters would have to get back on the train and try to return to the place where the nuns took Rudite to the hospital. No one was quite sure exactly where the hospital was but Erna said that the sisters assured her that they would find it. They were very brave and again risked being bombed while on the train, in order to help her reunite with her little girl.

Of course Erna was overjoyed that her baby would soon be joining them, since she missed her terribly. She nervously waited, almost afraid to take a breath, for the sisters' return. Unfortunately, when they returned it was without Rudite, and Erna's heart sank.

The sisters explained, "Her fever came back and the nuns would not let her come with us."

Two or three weeks went by and again they received a message that Rudite was better but very weak . There never was an explanation given for her illness. Again the sisters went to get her from the nuns and this time they were able to bring her back to her anxious mother. Finally Erna had both of her little girls again.

This was a very hard time for the Pottersdam refugees to endure. Erna remembered the constant air raids, the bombing, crying people, children getting sick and often dying. There were several children in the room that Erna's family shared. A little boy came down with measles and was put in quarantine. Erna worried, wondering what would happen to her little girls. Astride came down with the measles. After she recovered from the measles she contracted whooping cough and coughed continually until she was blue. There was no medication to help her, but, once again, she eventually got better.

After that Rudite almost died with the measles, since they went inside of her instead of breaking out. The medical authorities wanted to put her in quarantine, telling Erna that there was no hope for her.

The nurse, the sisters' mother, told Erna, "Don't cry. I will help you with her, you do not have to put her in quarantine." To put a child in quarantine was the equivalent of giving up, of accepting that the child was going to die.

With renewed hope Erna informed them, " No, she will stay with me."

In the middle of the night Rudite stopped breathing. The nurse administered CPR until she was revived. Throughout their children's illnesses Arijs did not help, seeming not to care about his children. He just sat in the corner playing cards with the other men, which is perhaps what men tended to do in those circumstances. They were powerless to do what society, throughout history, expected men to do – to provide and protect. As refugees they could not work and they could not fight so they often withdrew.

Finally, Rudite's condition improved. Erna hoped and prayed that they were done with sickness.

One day in December Erna recalled that "some guy" stopped in their room and said, "You know it is Christmas."

Christmas came but there was no way to celebrate it. They were just lucky to be alive. Thankfully, there was an organization that sent food packages with milk and other provisions for the children.

Astride, Rudite and Erna
Pottersdam - March 1945

11.

1945-1946

Beginnings And Endings

Pottersdam

THE NEW YEAR, 1945, arrived and no one knew what would happen.
The war was still going strong. Erna just hoped that they could stay in
Czechoslovakia since it was getting close to her due date. As that day
approached she was becoming very uncomfortable. She was also, understandably, worried because she had no idea where there was a hospital,
how far away it was and how she would get there. The sisters told her not
to worry, that they would locate it and take her to the hospital. Their
mother, the nurse, promised to help with the little girls while she was
gone.

Miraculously, despite all of the bombing, Erna made it to the hospital
in time and Zaiga Arija was born at 8:00 A.M., February 6,1945, right in

the middle of some very heavy bombing. There was no time to clean Erna or the new infant after the delivery. The mid-wives immediately took the mothers and newborns to a bomb shelter where they remained until late afternoon. Half

Pottersdam school house complex

of the town had been bombed and destroyed. Erna was sick with worry about her two little girls, Astride and Rudite, until she received word from the sisters that they were safe and unharmed. The school where they all lived had not been hit.

After all of the excitement of giving birth amidst the bombing, it suddenly occurred to Erna that she had no baby clothes for Zaiga. While rushing to pack her one suitcase for the boat she did not think about clothes for the baby that she was expecting. Five days passed and it was time for the mother and infant to be released, from the hospital. Of course she was very anxious to return to her family and thankfully, with her discharge, the hospital presented her with a package from the Red Cross. It contained baby clothes, including 6 cloth diapers that would need washing all of the time. Erna was grateful and thought to herself, " Good luck always follows me."

She explained how she coped during those times, "Scary, unexpected things would happen but I would just tell myself, don't worry, it will get better."

During February and March the bombing was relatively light, but in April it intensified. A good portion of the refugees' time was spent running to the bomb shelter. One time during very heavy bombing, as they crouched inside their shelter, the immense impact of the bombs threw several heavy metal doors against the entrance to their shelter, completely blocking it. Erna, her family, and the other refugees could not leave. Small children and grown people were crying in panic. Trapped there all night without any food or water, they did not know if they would ever get out. Finally, the next morning, they were rescued by German soldiers who were able to pry away the heavy doors.

The incessant bombing continued every day, which meant many trips to the bomb shelter, with the fear of being trapped again looming over them. On one occasion as the air raid warning sounded again, Astride sat on her bed and declared, " I am sitting right here. You can go if you want with Rudite and baby but I am staying."

Erna sat beside her on the bed, taking her in her arms, and replying, "No, if you are staying here than I am too."

The mother, holding her infant, Zaiga, sat there on the bed with her other two little girls snuggled next to her, as the bombs went off around them. Even though their building was hit, the half of the building where they were staying was not damaged, while the other half was destroyed. Erna remembered that day as again proof that basically she was a lucky person.

Several years later, when they were finally safe in the United States, Astride would hide under her bed whenever she would hear a plane fly over. This was one aspect of the war that Astride could never forget. Even as an adult she would panic if they were near airfields where there would be planes constantly landing and taking off. Understandably, she still refuses to watch any war movies.

The Red Cross, shortly after Zaiga was born, had come to visit them and had brought a baby carriage. That was truly a blessing. It gave Zaiga a place to sleep while they all went outside for walks in the fresh air, which the little girls loved to do. The Salvation Army would also bring cookies; candy and milk for the children, small treats that helped them survive the hard times.

Everyday the refugees hoped that tomorrow would be better. Everyone wondered how long they were going to be there. Then, on May 10, 1945, they heard that the war had ended and the refugees began to dare to dream, even perhaps planning to return to Latvia. But on that same evening their new dreams of hope were shattered when they looked out of their windows to see Russian soldiers and tanks once again filling the streets. The refugees had all run from the Russians when they took over Latvia and now, there they were again, since Czechoslovakia happened to fall in the Russian zone.

The Latvian refugee's worst nightmare was happening; to again be under Russian domination would be unbearable. That evening a young Latvian man, who was a friend of Janis, approached Erna. She had known him as a chauffeur in Latvia, working near where she lived. He was a good mechanic and knew a lot about fixing trucks.

"I have found a German truck with gas. Bring your kids, husband, and the clothing you need at 1:00 A.M... We will try to escape." He also warned, "The kids have to be very quiet."

Erna remembered," I thought to myself, what can I lose? I will die one way or another," she asked her husband what he thought and he said "Yes, we are going."

He left to help the young man work on the truck to get it running; probably feeling that at last there was something that he could do that was useful.

Erna packed their necessities into the baby carriage, secured all of her jewelry in a purse on a chain round her neck, and once again left a box full of belongings behind. That night they went quickly and quietly to the German truck. There were two families, altogether 11 people. They stood in the back of the truck, not making a sound. Erna was thankful for the baby carriage where Zaiga slept, snuggled under their coats and blankets. She constantly checked to make sure that her baby was not being suffocated.

The small group left at 1:00 A.M. because they knew that the Russian soldiers had been drinking all night and would be in an inebriated stupor. The driver had a map and knew exactly where to go. At about 7:00 A.M. they arrived in Germany at the American zone, and were stopped by American soldiers.

At first the soldiers could not understand why the Latvian refugees would want to leave the Russian zone, "Why do you want to leave? The Russians are on our side. They are just like us."

The soldiers were going to send them back, but luckily Erna could speak English and explained to them, "No. You don't know what they are like. They took all of our property. They have killed thousands of innocent Latvians and sent thousands to Siberia! If you send us back we will be shot or sent to Siberia! We cannot live under Communism!"

The soldiers listened to Erna and then told her group, "Wait here, we need to talk to our commander." After consulting with their commander they returned and asked Erna, "How many children are with you?"

The refugees were given food and milk and sent to a temporary shelter in an old school house until further arrangements could be made for them. Having traveled all through the night, the children were very tired. The adults didn't need much, they were just happy to have the milk for the children.

Esslingen Germany

After two to three days, the Red Cross arrived and made arrangements to transfer their group to a permanent Latvian refugee camp in Esslingen, Germany. Erna was relieved and happy to know that she would not be sent away to any more places. They were told to get their belongings together and were transported by truck to a train. For Erna, this time was a pleasant train ride, without the constant bombing, that took place during her last trip by train. She looked at the buildings as they passed and wondered where she would stay.

When they arrived at their destination in Esslingen, Germany, they were once again transported by truck to a large apartment building complex that surrounded a grassy area. Erna could not believe how beautiful it was. Her family was given a large apartment and only had to share the kitchen with one other lady. They had two rooms all to themselves. There was already a crib there for Zaiga and beds for Astride and Rudite. Conveniently, just a block from the camp was a Latvian School. It was more than she could possibly have hoped for. Life had started to get a little bit better.

Ironically, she found out later that her good fortune had come on the backs of others' misfortune. The apartments had been occupied, before the war, by Jewish families who had been arrested and deported to concentration camps, leaving behind all of their belongings.

With three small children to support and no employment, Erna wondered what she could do to earn money. While she was watching her little girls playing in the sandbox and worrying about her economic situation, another refugee lady approached her. "I see that you have small children. They must keep you busy."

Erna agreed and shared her concerns, "I don't know how I will get enough money to buy them shoes."

The lady smiled, "That is why I came to talk to you. If you can knit you can make some money. The camp organization will pay for your work. They pay by the weight of the yarn."

Erna replied, "It isn't my strongest skill but I can learn." She had always preferred crocheting and embroidery but now she described herself as "a very happy camper". She could knit while her little girls played in the sand box and Zaiga napped in the baby carriage.

Life had improved for Erna and her family. Astride was happy to spend part of her day in school learning Latvian and German. Erna, knowing how important it was to learn these languages, also provided private English lessons for her older daughter in an evening adult class conducted by a friend. Most of all, Astride was thrilled to receive, every so often, a little box, its top decorated with a red cross. Inside the box were school supplies, a toothbrush, tooth paste and a can of Hershey's liquid chocolate, which was a new treat for Astride. The item in the box that she found the most exciting was a No.2 pencil. Before this, she had always used ink to do her schoolwork. Now the No.2 pencil was, to her, a miraculous treasure.

In the fall Erna became ill. She thought that it was the flu but when she didn't get better she went to the doctor. If she was seriously ill she wondered who would take care of her children.

The doctor informed her that she was pregnant and said, "God wanted you to have more children."

After she returned home she cried for several hours, then took a deep breath, and told herself, "You have to take what life dishes out." a lesson that she had already learned many times.

Winter approached and Erna again wondered how she was going to earn money to buy shoes and warm clothes for her little girls.

The same lady, who had given her the knitting job, again sought Erna out and told her, "I have found some discarded parachutes by the garbage. The parachutes are made from light green and light blue silk. We need to get them unraveled and washed. There is a shortage of women's lingerie right now. I can make patterns for slips and nightgowns. I will sew them, then you can embroider designs on them." she explained.

Erna and her friend unraveled and washed the parachutes. The friend was an accomplished seamstress and made a pattern for slips and nightgowns. She would then cut out and sew the garments. While her children slept at night, Erna would happily embroider the lingerie with beautiful flowers and intricate borders. As a child Erna had loved embroidering, describing it as "painting with thread". Now that skill was helping her take care of her children.

Most of the time Arijs was absent, having secured employment as a truck driver that delivered food for UNDRA. Erna never knew where he was. As her due date approached she had to think about how she would get to the hospital. The lady next door helped Erna find a German girl, Anna Wagner, who would love to look after the children while she was in the hospital.

"Once again Lady Luck knocked at my door." Erna recalled.

On June 28, 1946, Anna came to stay with Zaiga, Rudite and Astride, since Erna's contractions had begun. Without anyone to accompany her, she took the street car to the hospital. The hospital was so crowded that she gave birth to her fourth daughter, Inara, at 10:00 P.M. that evening, in the hallway. After three days, she and her new baby girl returned home on the streetcar. Anna reported that while Erna was away, Astride was like a little mother, helping Rudite get dressed and looking after Zaiga.

Reunions And Separations

One evening, after Erna and the new baby were settled back in their apartment, there was a knock on the door. Erna opened it cautiously and was amazed to see her father standing there. She had no idea what had happened to him, but remembered his last words to her when they were separated in Poland, "When the war is over, I will find you."

He had been working for the U.S. Army Corps of Engineers and had met some other Latvian refugees who had visited Erna's camp.

Janis in Germany

They told him "There is a young Latvian mother with four little girls living in the camp at Esslingen."

Janis knew immediately that it had to be Erna and said, "That is my daughter."

Having her father nearby again was a blessing for Erna since she never saw her husband. Now there was one other person that she could rely on, not just herself. Janis took over the maintenance of the compound, which included the important task of maintaining the heating system.

In the fall of 1946, Erna decided that she would try to have her two babies, Zaiga and Inara, baptized in the Lutheran Church. A Latvian couple, who came to visit from the English camp, offered to ask their Lutheran minister if he would perform the ceremony.

Zaiga and Inara's (held) Christening
The two children in the very front from the right: Astride and Rudite
Germany - September 1946

The minister replied, "I will be delighted to baptize the babies."

When he came for the ceremony Erna was surprised to see that it was the minister who had presided at her marriage to Arijs.

After the baptism the minister observed to Erna, "I noticed that your husband was not here for the baptism."

At first she thought that she would just say that he was too busy driving truck for UNDRA, but then she looked at the man who had married them and realized that she could not lie.

With a great deal of embarrassment, she confessed to the minister, "My husband and I are not living together. He has met another woman and has nothing to do with us anymore."

The minister was furious and took it upon himself to hunt down Arijs and admonish him for abandoning his family, reminding him, "You were married in the church and took a vow to love your wife until death do you part."

Arijs returned in a rage and confronted Erna, "So why did you complain to the minister about me? What were you thinking to embarrass me in this way?"

He began to hit her repeatedly and pushed her with so much force that she fell backwards, hitting her head and hurting her back. One of the neighbors eventually found her and took her to the hospital.

The next day Astride, concerned about her mama, found her way to the hospital. She was only 6 years old but walked, by herself, across the city. She crossed a huge, busy bridge that divided the city and then walked up the hill to the hospital in Esslingen.

On her way she would stop people and ask them, "Where is the hospital? How do I get to the hospital from here?"

Erna remembered waking, disoriented, in her hospital room, and seeing Astride by her bedside. She said that at first she thought that she was looking at an angel.

"Astride, honey, how did you get here?" she asked.

"I walked, Mama. I wanted to see how you were."

Erna talked to the nuns at the hospital and they agreed to make arrangements to safely return Astride to their apartment. She still worries that Astride never had a childhood. Born with an old soul, Astride looked after her little sisters, helped her mother, and was wise beyond her years. At such a young age she seemed to accept their situation and did everything that she could to make it better.

Erna described that painful time, "There was nothing that I could do. There was no protection for women then. Everyone just felt that it was not their business."

This is the part of the story that at first was not going to be revealed. Erna had never talked to her daughters about it. She felt that Astride was the only one who might have been aware of the abuse since she was the oldest and very little got past her attention. Like so many women who suffer abuse at the hands of their husbands, there is a certain amount of undeserved shame that they feel. Erna decided that at age 96, she was finally going to tell the truth about this part of her life. She had survived and escaped the Russians twice. She had lived through bombings and near starvation, while keeping her children safe. She was in the Free World, but still had to fear her husband. Ironically, Erna and Janis had risked their lives carrying the injured Arijs with them in the wagon when they fled Latvia. She could not understand what had changed him. He had not been abusive at first. She supposed that it was the war. The war took its toll in many ways, not just in battles. It was a very bitter pill for Erna to swallow.

When Christmas arrived that year there, again, was no tree with candles at the apartment, but Santa Claus came with toys for the children. They could hear people singing Christmas carols throughout the camp. It was their first Christmas in the Free World. There were no communists, so no one had to worry about what would happen to them if they celebrated Christmas.

12.

1947-1948

Difficult Times

Illnesses and Transfers

THEY CONTINUED TO LIVE one day at a time, waiting and wondering about their immigration status. Everything seemed to be going fine until the baby, Inara, developed a stomach problem. Nothing seemed to help. Finally, in desperation, Erna wrapped her baby in a blanket and accompanied by the camp director, took Inara to the nearest hospital in Stuttgart.

The nuns at the hospital told her, "There is not much hope. You need to go back to your apartment and take care of your other children."

Erna had already made arrangements with her neighbor to take care of her three little girls and refused to leave. She stayed there with Inara for several days until the nuns finally convinced her that her baby was improving enough for her to go home to rest.

Inara, struggling to live, remained in the hospital for 6 months. Erna visited her every day and recalled that her baby seemed to know when her mother would be coming. When she walked into the hospital room the first thing that Erna would see was her baby's sweet little face waiting and watching for her.

As Inara's health improved, the nuns tried to convince Erna to give her baby to them. "You have three little girls at home. Your hands are full and you have so many burdens since your husband has left you."

Erna was appalled. Did they think that they could make Inara a nun or put her up for adoption? There was no way that she would ever give up any of her children, having struggled so hard to keep them alive.

On Inara's first birthday, Erna went to the hospital, dressed her baby in a beautiful white dress, that she had sewn especially for that day, and took her home. There was only enough money to take the streetcar part way. The rest of the trip home she walked, carrying her little girl. Erna had baked a cake before she left for the hospital, so that when she and Inara arrived home, the family would celebrate their baby's first birthday and homecoming.

Then it was Astride's turn to be ill. She started to run a very high fever. The Latvian doctor that Erna had consulted before she left Latvia happened to be in the same camp.

He examined Astride and said, "Astride has an infection in her lungs. There is no medicine available and since she is getting worse I will try a treatment that will be extremely painful. Astride will have to be very brave and strong."

He Placed hot suction cups on her back to try to loosen the infection in her lungs. The suction cups left red marks and scars but Astride, as stoic as ever, never complained. Erna worried what Immigration someday might do if they saw those marks. Would they reject Astride as not being healthy enough?

The doctor thought that Astride would benefit from living in a wooded area with lots of pine trees. Erna received permission to relocate to a camp in Karlsruhe that was near a forest.

At the camp in Karlsruhe they shared a house with a woman who was a dentist. Erna was able to work in the kitchen in the morning while the little ones were in preschool and Astride and Rudite were in school. Zaiga needed shoes and now Erna had earned enough money to buy her beautiful, sturdy brown high tops.

The only problem with living in the forest was that there were swarms of mosquitoes and the old German barracks had no window screens. For some reason those mosquitoes only feasted on Astride, covering her legs and arms with huge welts. Erna tried covering the welts with bandages but that did not help. Finally Astride was so miserable that she announced "I can't take this anymore!"

Erna asked for permission to transfer back to their previous camp in Esslingen, which, unfortunately, was where her husband and his girlfriend were living. She also wanted to enroll her children in school. Luckily there was an opening for them in Sillenbuch. This was ideal because that camp was near enough to Esslingen so that Janis could visit his family often, but not in the same camp as Arijs and his girlfriend.

On the day that they were ready to relocate to Sillenbuch, Erna realized that Zaiga was missing a shoe. It seemed that Zaiga did not appreciate the new shoes because she preferred to be barefoot. Erna frantically searched everywhere, inside and outside, with no luck. There was no more time to look; they had to leave, minus a shoe. Erna was so worried about how she would get the money to replace them that she started to sob, "Not much could make me cry, but I broke down in tears when I could not find that shoe."

Once situated in Sillenbach, Erna enrolled the girls in school, where she was able to work in the kindergarten room. With her earnings she could afford to buy Astride skis, plus shoes for all of the girls. That winter Astride skied and the little ones went sledding. Happily, Janis was in Esslingen, close enough to visit them on the weekends.

13.

1949

Immigration

Last Displaced Person Camp

THROUGHOUT THEIR TIME as refugees in Germany, Erna had been thinking about where she would like to live. She knew that she did not want to remain in Germany and remembered that Janis had always advised her to try to get to the United States. Shortly after the start of the New Year, after they had relocated in Sillenbuch, there was a knock on her door. She opened the door to a Quaker gentleman who brought good news from the United States. This gentleman was sent by Arijs's Uncle John, who lived in the U.S. The uncle was a Quaker and had been working with the Quaker Church, the Society of Friends, to try to locate his nephew and his family. He wanted to help them relocate to the United States.

Janis

The Quaker gentleman asked Erna, "Where is your husband, Arijs?"

"He is not here right now. He drives a truck for UNDRA, delivering food," she replied. "When he returns I will be sure to tell him the good news."

Of course he was living with his new girlfriend, but Erna did not want the Quaker gentleman to know that. She discussed the problem with Janis. This would be her family's best chance to get to the United States with the help of the Quakers and her husband's uncle. She was going to need her husband's cooperation.

Janis told her, "Do what you have to do."

He contacted her husband for her. Arijs agreed to reunite and move the family to Esslingen in order to be able to emigrate. He had no intention of giving up the girlfriend, still spending most of his time with her.

"Once we get to the United States we will see what happens," was all that he would promise.

Unfortunately with their return to Esslingen the beatings resumed. One time, in a rage, he beat Erna because she refused to give him a gold mesh bracelet that her father had given her. Arijs wanted to sell it in order to support his life. Erna kept her jewelry in a small change purse on a chain around her neck at all times and would not part with it. It was her security in case of an emergency.

The Quaker gentleman, on one of his visits, noticed her black eye, "What happened to your eye?" He asked with concern.

"Oh, I am so clumsy. I tripped and fell." She told him, offering the most frequent explanation of a battered woman.

The weather, during that first summer, after returning to Esslingen, was exceptionally hot. On Sundays a truck would take the children and their parents to the river to swim and play.

The other mothers encouraged Erna, "Come with us and bring your little girls. They will love playing in the water."

Erna

On one especially hot Sunday afternoon, Erna decided to join the group and take her children to the river. She sat beside the river, watching her four little girls having a wonderful time as they played in the water and on the river's bank. When it was time to go, Zaiga could not be found. Erna could not imagine where her little girl could be, since she had just been watching her play with the others. She started calling for her. Everyone helped her search. The police were summoned, and they began looking for her in the water, afraid that she may have drowned. Erna kept walking along the river's edge, back and forth, refusing to leave.

Finally, everyone left, but Erna stayed. "There was no way that I would leave not knowing where my child was."

At last, she discovered Zaiga, curled up, contentedly sleeping under a bridge. Erna remembered, "Someone gave us a ride back to camp."

Perhaps on that day Erna understood how frightened her own parents must have been when she decided to take a nap in a coffin, years ago.

While they waited in Esslingen for the paperwork to go through for the immigration to the U.S., Uncle John sent them care packages with coffee and food. Janis stopped smoking so that he could contribute his cigarettes that the army gave him. Erna would take the coffee and cigarettes to a farm and trade them for vegetables to feed her children.

Astride

On one of those trips to the farm she was stopped by the military police that inspected what she was carrying.

"Where are you going with those cigarettes? Are you selling them on the Black Market?" they asked.

"No. I am not trying to get money for them. I just want to trade them for fresh vegetables for my children." She explained.

Luckily, they believed her and let her continue on her way. This was another instance when her ability to speak English was very beneficial.

Near the camp, along the road, grew many apple trees. The refugees were allowed to pick all of the apples that they could use as they ripened. Erna and her children took a large basket and filled it with apples. She remembered how much she enjoyed that delicious fruit. She cooked with them, baked apple bread, ate them right off of the tree, and dried apple slices on long strings to eat later. As a service to the refugees, the bakeries in town would leave their ovens on at the end of day, when their baking was done, and allow the refugees to come in and bake their bread.

Inara

Waiting For Immigration

As they continued to wait in Esslingen, during the long and complicated process of being able to immigrate to the U.S., Erna sold the rest of the diamonds from the watch that had been her confirmation gift. She had the diamonds replaced with some artificial stones that resembled diamonds, and with the money from those diamonds she paid for English language lessons and piano lessons for Astride. Many of the refugees were professionals; doctors, opera singers, musicians, nurses, dentists and artists. They were displaced people, hoping to find a new life, and doing what they could to survive.

With her "diamond money" Erna was also able to purchase material for her children's clothing, which her neighbor helped her sew. She was aware that some of the people at the camp were probably speculating and gossiping as to how she acquired the money for those lessons and clothes but she didn't care. She understood how important the ability to speak English was going to be for Astride when she started school in the U.S.

The Quaker gentleman kept in touch with them and visited often. He had fallen in love with Erna's beautiful little girls and was very surprised and impressed at how well Astride could speak English.

Their long wait came to an end toward the end of August, 1949, with the arrival of the letter that instructed them to get ready to go to the United States. There wasn't much to pack; just some blankets, some pictures, their clothing. While they waited Erna made the traditional Latvian costumes for her daughters.

1949 - Girls wearing traditional Latvian costumes. Astride wearing Grandmother's amber necklace.

She used U.S. army blankets. The army green color was perfect for Rudite's and Zaiga's costumes. She needed to dye one of the blankets black for Astride's outfit. Her neighbor, who was a seamstress, (and previously had been an opera singer in Latvia) helped her acquire the black dye and also helped her dye the blanket. Procuring the ribbons was a problem. Erna found some red tape that would suffice, and was able to buy some ribbons on the black market. Using money from her "watch diamonds" to buy the linen for the blouses, she then embroidered the blouses, using darning thread, since she could not find real embroidery thread. She was able to borrow a crown, Latvian jewelry, and Inara's costume, since she was running out of time trying to complete all of the costumes.

1948 - Girls wearing traditional Latvian costumes before emigration

There were photographers who would come through the camps and offer to take pictures of the families. A photograph of the four little girls in their costumes was taken. Erna still proudly displays that framed picture on her wall today. For Erna, making those costumes was her last connection to Latvia, a way to honor the country that she loved and perhaps would never see again. Each stitch was a tribute to her brother, her mother and her grandfather, who were still held captive in Siberia.

1949 - Clinton Farm

Sadly, Erna was going to have to leave her father once again. Janis told her, "Don't worry. I will be all right. I will get to the United States with the help of the Lutheran Church."

She promised him, "When I get to the United States I will do everything that I can to help you get there."

In late September she received the letter telling her that they would be sailing to the United States on October 1, 1949. She said, "that letter ended one time in my life."

Janis went with them to the train. As she and her little girls boarded the train, she promised her father, "I will see you soon."

Her father stood on the platform, tears streaming down his face, waving goodbye. The little girls were waving and calling "Grandpa!"

The train transported them to the Port. At the port they boarded the ship, the USS General C.H. Muir for their transatlantic voyage. As they boarded, the men were separated from the women and children.

Unfortunately, October is notably the worst time to sail since the sea becomes very rough. Erna, Rudite, Zaiga and Inara were miserably sea sick. Astride, for some reason, was not sea sick, and worried about her mother and little sisters. She did her best to take care of them, bringing them oranges and food. The voyage seemed to take forever.

At last on Oct.10, 1949, they arrived in New York Harbor in the evening. Over the loudspeaker, the captain announced to everyone, "Look. There is the Statue of Liberty!"

It was all lit up, "just like a fairy tale." When she saw the statue Erna knew that they were finally safe. Erna and her family disembarked at Ellis Island. She retrieved her possessions which had been placed into a large green box, labeled with her family's name. Astride's Teddy bear was in the box with their other possessions, but he was not allowed to accompany them any further. The authorities confiscated the Teddy bear, since stuffed toys were not allowed to enter. Astride had carried that Teddy with her from Latvia to Czechoslovakia and finally to Germany, but she would not be able to carry him into the United States.

They were directed into lines for the medical exam and inoculations. Erna had worried about Astride's lungs, but everyone passed.

At the gate the Quaker gentleman was waiting for them. From there they took a train to Detroit where they would temporarily stay with a Quaker family. On the train Erna had only one dime. She said, "I did not know what I would do when I got there, but one thing that I did know, we were free."

In reflection, Erna remarked that "1945- 1949 were only 4 years, actually a short time in one's life, but so much happened in those four years, some good and some bad."

*Arrival in USA.
Astride, Rudite,
Zaiga and Inara*

Janice Whelan and Erna P. Roberts

Epilogue

This is one refugee of war whose story will not be lost. Erna's love for her daughters caused her to dig deeply into the memories that she had stored away and retrieve for them the story of her past and their beginnings. It is one young woman's story but it also tells the story of the innocent victims of war, the women and children. It is the timeless story of people forced from their land, stripped of everything that they have owned who are able to not just survive but triumph over what seemed to be insurmountable obstacles. It is the story of a father and daughter and how their deep love for each other sustained and empowered them. It is the story of the strength of one woman's courage in her struggle to keep her young daughters alive. And it is the story of how women in adversity band together and help each other out. Men who become displaced by war often feel powerless since they are used to working, solving problems and fighting. They are the protectors and providers and when they can't do that, they often do not know what to do. Women, used to often being powerless are the caregivers, knowing how to nurture and protect and how to scrape for what they and their children need. Many, like Erna, become fierce protectors and risk takers in order to care for their babies.

Once in the U.S., not wanting to raise her daughters in the city, Erna chose to settle with the Quakers' assistance in a small rural town, Clinton, Michigan. Later she was able to get a job at the Tecumseh Products. Jens Touberg, one of the founders of Tecumseh Products, a Danish immigrant, and his wife, were strong advocates for Erna. They even accompanied her to court during her divorce proceedings. Since she and Arijs were not yet citizens it was a very difficult divorce and took an entire day to get through it. Her husband, once in the United States, had chosen to live in Ohio on the weekends with his girlfriend. His uncle had also paid for her immigration.

Eventually, at work, she met Jerry Roberts, a widower. They married, and later her daughters took his last name legally when they became citizens at age 18. They had 6 children in their combined family, since Jerry had a son and daughter of his own.

Zaiga, Astride and Inara

Janis was able to join them in 1951, quietly living with Erna and Jerry. He was not in good health but enjoyed taking care of Jens Touberg's orchard. It was ironic and also sad that one of the most influential and wealthy men of Latvia was doing landscaping in the United States. Erna never disclosed her past to anyone. Consequently, everyone referred to Janis as "Mrs. Robert's dad."

Janis died on Dec. 17, 1961, still wondering if his son and his wife were alive. He knew that they were confined in Siberia but never made contact with them for fear that he would cause them problems. He said that they had suffered enough already.

After her father's death, Ray Herrick (President of Tecumseh Products) called her into his office. Erna was very

Inara and Grandfather Janis, in Tecumseh MI

nervous and wondered what she had done to get his attention. He was holding a newspaper clipping from a Chicago paper. The article was titled "Ex-Latvian Millionaire dies in Tecumseh".

Ex-Latvian Millionaire Dies in Tecumseh

Silent on Origin in Fear of Reds

Tecumseh - (Special) - Death has ended the anonymity of Janis Murmanis, 74-year-old Latvian.

Fear of reprisal gone now, he was revealed Friday as a former multimillionaire who was the biggest commercial and industrial building contractor in Latvia until World War II.

He died Thursday at the home of his daughter, Mrs. Gerald Roberts of Tecumseh, with whom he had made his home since coming to the United States in 1951.

He died still wondering whether his wife, Pauline, and son, Zigfried, are alive. The last he knew, both were confined in a Russian prison camp in Siberia.

When the Russians took over Latvia they tried to persuade him to go to Russia to continue his work as a contractor for them. When he refused he was forced to flee his homeland, leaving his wife and son.

Mrs. Roberts, the former Erna Murmanis, who was first married before the war, also escaped from Latvia with her seven children, but her husband was killed. She came to the United States and married Mr. Roberts, a design engineer at the Tecumseh Products Co.

Mr. Murmanis was rescued by the Allied forces and was employed as a civilian in charge of all U. S. Army barracks construction in Germany after World War II.

He learned that his wife and son were prisoners in Siberia and that his daughter had escaped to the United States. But he could not join her here until 1951, when he was allowed to enter the country under the displaced persons quota.

Since then he has been known by most Tecumseh area residents only as Mrs. Roberts' father.

Services will be conducted Saturday at 2 p.m. in the Collins-Corkery Funeral Home with burial in Brookside, Tecumseh.

Mr. Herrick asked, "Why didn't you tell us who you were?"

Erna replied, "That life is over and I saw no reason to talk about it."

To this day Erna is perplexed as to who wrote that article and how they got the information. Most of the information was correct except for the part stating that she and Jerry had 7 children and that her first husband had died in Latvia.

In 1965, a cousin in Latvia, Zidra, contacted Erna. Her mother and brother had been located in Siberia with the help of the Red Cross, using the list of displaced persons. Erna actually fainted when she heard the news, something that she had never done. In 1968 they were released to Latvia, but were not allowed to live in Ligatne at that time. They were sent to another town, Talsi, by the Russian government, but did return to the Ligatne area.

Erna's husband Jerry died suddenly in 1971. Shortly after his death she received permission to go to Riga in Latvia for 10 days, to visit her mother and brother. She had not seen them since the day when they were on the box car, being exiled to Siberia. On that day, her brother was a teenager and her mother a much younger woman. At their reunion, her mother was an old woman with a cane and her brother was a middle aged man. Erna could not believe what she was seeing.

Cousin Arvid, wife Vilma, Erna, Pauline, brother Zigfrids, and wife Zigrida
Reunion in Latvia - 1971

But then her mother said, "I can't understand why Erna doesn't have a hat."

Yes, that was the mother she remembered, the lady who loved her hats and shoes. Her mother was afraid that Erna was too poor to have a hat. Neither Pauline nor Zigfrids would talk about their lives in Siberia. They would just say, "Don't ask. Don't talk about the past." Even now her brother does not want to talk about the Latvia that they once knew and what happened to them during those lost years.

*Erna and Pauline (mother)
in Latvia*

On the second and third trip to Latvia Astride traveled with Erna and was able to see her grandmother twice. Ray Herrick became interested and wanted to bring Pauline to the United States. Unfortunately, in 1980, Pauline became ill and Erna was denied permission to enter Latvia. She was not able to return until 1995, long after her mother had died. Zigfrids told her that the orchestra played at her mother's funeral, using the instruments that her father had donated to the community before the war. Zigfrids also told Erna that he had bought her first teacher's piano. Pauline was buried in the family plot in Ligatne.

Throughout the war Janis was able to save all of the papers that proved his ownership of the factories, land and businesses. Erna has no idea how he was able to do that considering all that he had been through during the war. Perhaps they were hidden in a secret compartment in that brown brief case that was always with him.

When he came to the United States he gave his daughter those papers and said, "Keep these in a safe place, perhaps they will be useful some day."

After the Soviet Union fell, and Latvia was once again independent, Erna took the papers to Zigfrids, signing them over to him. "I had no need of the property and he went through too much." The woodworking Ligatne factory is back in their ownership, and today it is operated by Zigfrid's grandson. Most of the property was returned, except for the machinery, house and stable.

During several trips back to Latvia, family pictures were collected from relatives who had survived the war years.

The maids, who worked for Erna's family before the war, stayed in Latvia. Through the years they watched over the property, even hiding some of Pauline's china and crystal. Years later when Astride and her husband visited, they ate dinner on her grandmother's dishes.

Erna

Erna's new life in the United States was not without tragedy. First, she lost her husband, Jerry. Then her youngest daughter, Inara, became very ill. After many years of poor health, she died in 2006. No parent expects to outlive their children. The loss of Inara was a terrible blow to Erna and she misses her greatly.

Today, Erna is a beautiful woman with soft snowy white hair and large blue eyes. She is still able to take brisk walks in her neighborhood. At 96, Erna has her own apartment and is proudly self sufficient, although she is a little frustrated with her diminishing eyesight. Her hearing is very sharp as is her mind, since she is still able to converse in three languages. For many years, after she retired from the Products, she owned a yarn shop in Adrian, Michigan, and still knits Christmas stockings and blankets for her great grandchildren, whom she adores.

She spends 6 months out of the year in Pennsylvania with her daughter Astride, going there in the spring, so that she can plant and care for their flowers throughout the summer. She takes pleasure in her quiet life, probably reminding herself of what she continually told herself throughout the war, "You have to take what life gives you."

Erna has a family in Latvia and three daughters, ten grandchildren and 22 great grandchildren scattered across the United States with a Latvian heritage.

Janice Whelan and Erna P. Roberts

Made in the USA
Middletown, DE
08 December 2015